Los Angeles Angels 2019

A Baseball Companion

Edited by Patrick Dubuque, Aaron Gleeman and Bret Sayre

Baseball Prospectus

Craig Brown and Dave Pease, Consultant Editors
Rob McQuown and Harry Pavlidis, Statistics Editors

Copyright © 2019 by DIY Baseball, LLC.
All rights reserved

This book or any part thereof may not be reproduced or transmitted in any form or by any means, electronic or mechanical, including photocopying, recording, or by any information storage and retrieval system, without permission in writing from the publisher.

Limit of Liability/Disclaimer of Warranty: While the publisher and the author have used their best efforts in preparing this book, they make no representations or warranties with respect to the accuracy or completeness of the contents of this book and specifically disclaim any implied warranties of merchantability or fitness for a particular purpose. No warranty may be created or extended by sales representatives or written sales materials. The advice and strategies contained herein may not be suitable for your situation. You should consult with a professional where appropriate. Neither the publisher nor the author shall be liable for any loss of profit or any other commercial damages, including but not limited to special, incidental, consequential, or other damages.

Library of Congress Cataloging-in-Publication Data:
paperback
ISBN-13: 978-1-949332-14-8

Project Credits
Cover Design: Kathleen Dyson
Interior Design and Production: Jeff Pease, Dave Pease
Layout: Jeff Pease, Dave Pease

Baseball icon courtesy of Uberux, from https://www.shareicon.net/author/uberux

Ballpark diagram courtesy of Lou Spirito/THIRTY81 Project, https://thirty81project.com/

Manufactured in the United States of America
10 9 8 7 6 5 4 3 2 1

Table of Contents

Foreword v
    Rob Mains

Statistical Introduction vii

Part 1: Team Analysis

Table for Two: Previewing the 2019 Los Angeles Angels 3
    Mark Barry and Ginny Searle

Performance Graphs 9

2018 Team Performance 10

2019 Team Projections 11

Team Personnel 12

Angel Stadium Stats 13

Angels Team Analysis 15

Part 2: Player Analysis

Angels Player Analysis 22

Angels Prospects 103

Part 3: Featured Articles

The Hole in The Shift is Fixing Itself 117
    Russell Carleton

The State of the Quality Start 121
    Rob Mains

Heads-Up Hacking—The First Pitch 127
    Matthew Trueblood

A Hymn for the Index Stat 133
    Patrick Dubuque

Index of Names 137

Foreword

Rob Mains

Welcome to this companion of the 2019 Los Angeles Angels. We at Baseball Prospectus are excited to provide this analysis of the Angels.

Our website, Baseball Prospectus, is a leader in delivering high-quality commentary and data to baseball fans everywhere. To some, those words—commentary and data—appear mutually exclusive. There are people out there who believe that traditional analysis and advanced analytics must run on different paths. But the simplistic narrative of stats vs. traditionalists just isn't true. Every team's analytics department interacts with scouting, development, and major league operations with a common goal: Delivering a championship. New technologies, like radar tracking of pitch speeds and movement, enable talent evaluators to focus on qualitative aspects of pitching like mechanics and pitch sequencing. In-game strategies like infield shifts, based on batters' hit tendencies, help turn balls in play into outs. Hitters use information to adjust their swings to maximize run production.

All these numbers can seem, at best, intimidating, and at worst, counterproductive to the casual fan. Even as technology and analysis have embedded themselves deeply into the way teams run, it can often feel like statistics create a displacement between the viewer and the sport, breaking them out of the action. And yet every fan incorporates the numbers to some degree; stats like batting average and earned run average, so fundamental to how we talk about performance, are actually complicated formulas. They don't bother people because those formulas have become second nature, as easy to translate as the action on the field.

Along the way, new statistics have entered baseball's lexicon. You'll see some of them, like on-base percentage (which measures a batter's ability to get on base via walk, hit batter, or hit), OPS (on-base plus slugging), and average exit velocity (the speed of balls off a hitter's bat) on broadcasts. Others, like DRC+, might well be new to you. Some of them have been well-defined to the public, others haven't. That lack of context has created ambiguity. Fans know that a ball hit 100 mph is scorched, but does that mean extra bases? (Not if it's hit on the ground or high in the air it doesn't.)

For those who are amenable to them, the new statistics can increase the enjoyment and understanding of the game. They can help fans identify when a pitcher is tiring, when a stolen base or a bunt attempt makes sense (and, more often, when it doesn't), or how a team's lineup might be constructed. Websites like Baseball Prospectus add to that understanding by weaving metrics into the narrative of the game. That's the goal of this publication: to take some of the newer, more complicated statistics and make them as intuitive as the ones on the back of old baseball cards.

But you don't need to love analytics to love baseball. The fans at BP who worked together to write this guide are captivated first and foremost by the game itself. We're drawn to Aaron Judge's power, Francisco Lindor's glove, Billy Hamilton's speed and Patrick Corbin's slider and don't need numbers to tell us why they're so mesmerizing. The underlying statistics provide depth to the game that we all love.

We hope you'll find that this guide helps you better understand the Angels. Our analysts have studied the team's major league personnel and its minor league affiliates to identify their strengths and weaknesses, both the obvious ones and those that only a careful dissection of players' performances—yes, including the data—can reveal. You don't need us to tell you who was good and who wasn't in 2018, but our models and writers can help you project how each player is going to perform this year and beyond, and appreciate the greatness of each new game as it unfolds. As in the sport itself, the human and analytic components combine to generate a deeper overall understanding.

Think back to the first time you saw a baseball game on a high-definition TV. You'd grown familiar with how the game looked and felt on a picture tube. But new TV allowed you to see details that you'd never seen before. That's how advanced statistics work. The game itself is why you're here and why you're buying this. (And, for that matter, why we wrote it.) The statistical measures provide the sharper focus, the detail, the depth of knowledge that you didn't have before, generating an overall superior picture. Enjoy the view.

—*Rob Mains is an author of Baseball Prospectus.*

Statistical Introduction

Sports are, fundamentally, a blend of athletic endeavor and storytelling. Baseball, like any other sport, tells its stories in so many ways: in the arc of a game from the stands or a season from the box scores, in photos, or even in numbers. At Baseball Prospectus, we understand that statistics don't replace observation or any of baseball's stories, but complement everything else that makes the game so much fun.

What stats help us with is with patterns and precision, variance and value. This book can help you learn things you may not see from watching a game or hundred, whether it's the path of a career over time or the breadth of the entire MLB. We'd also never ask you to choose between our numbers and the experience of viewing a game from the cheap seats or the comfort of your home; our publication combines running the numbers with observations and wisdom from some of the brightest minds we can find. But if you *do* want to learn more about the numbers beyond what's on the backs of player jerseys, let us help explain.

Offense

At the end of this past year, we've revised our methodology for determining batting value. Long-time readers of Baseball Prospectus will notice that we've retired True Average in favor of a new metric: Deserved Runs Created Plus (DRC+). Developed by Jonathan Judge and our stats team, this statistic measures everything a player does at the plate–reaching base, hitting for power, making outs, and moving runners over–and puts it on a scale where 100 equals league-average performance. A DRC+ of 150 is terrific, a DRC+ of 100 is average, and a DRC+ of 75 means you better be an excellent defender.

DRC+ also does a better job than any of our previous metrics in taking contextual factors into account. The model adjusts for how the park affects performance, but also for things like the talent of the opposing pitcher, value of different types of batted-ball events, league, temperature, and other factors. It's able to describe a player's expected offensive contribution than any other statistic we've found over the years, and also does a better job of predicting future performance as well.

The other aspect of run-scoring is baserunning, which we quantify using Baserunning Runs. BRR not only records the value of stolen bases (or getting caught in the act), but also accounts for a runner's ability to go first to third on a single or advance on a fly ball.

Defense

Where offensive value is *relatively* easy to identify and understand, defensive value is ... not. Over the past dozen years, the sabermetric community has focused mostly on stats based on zone data: a real-live human person records the type of batted ball and estimated landing location, and models are created that give expected outs. From there, you can compare fielders' actual outs to those expected ones. Simple, right?

Unfortunately, zone data has two major issues. First, zone data is recorded by commercial data providers who keep the raw data private unless you pay for it. (All the statistics we build in this book and on our website use public data as inputs.) That hurts our ability to test assumptions or duplicate results. Second, over the years it has become apparent that there's quite a bit of "noise" in zone-based fielding analysis. Sometimes the conclusions drawn from zone data don't hold up to scrutiny, and sometimes the different data provided by different providers don't look anything alike, giving wildly different results. Sometimes the hard-working professional stringers or scorers might unknowingly inflict unconscious bias into the mix: for example good fielders will often be credited with more expected outs despite the data, and ballparks with high press boxes tend to score more line drives than ones with a lower press box.

Enter our Fielding Runs Above Average (FRAA). For most positions, FRAA is built from play-by-play data, which allows us to avoid the subjectivity found in many other fielding metrics. The idea is this: count how many fielding plays are made by a given player and compare that to expected plays for an average fielder at their position (based on pitcher ground-ball tendencies and batter handedness). Then we adjust for park and base-out situations.

When it comes to catchers, our methodology is a little different thanks to the laundry list of responsibilities they're tasked with beyond just, well, catching and throwing the ball. By now you've probably heard about "framing" or the art of making umpires more likely to call balls outside the strike zone for strikes. To put this into one tidy number, we incorporate pitch tracking data (for the years it exists) and adjust for important factors like pitcher, umpire, batter, and home-field advantage using a mixed-model approach. This grants us a number for how many strikes the catcher is personally adding to (or subtracting from) his pitchers' performance ... which we then convert to runs added or lost using linear weights.

Framing is one of the biggest parts of determining catcher value, but we also take into account blocking balls from going past, whether a scorer deems it a passed ball or a wild pitch. We use a similar approach–one that really benefits from the pitch tracking data that tells us what ends up in the dirt and what doesn't. We also include a catcher's ability to prevent stolen bases and how well they field balls in play, and *finally* we come up with our FRAA for catchers.

Pitching

Both pitching and fielding make up the half of baseball that isn't run scoring: run prevention. Separating pitching from fielding is a tough task, and most recent pitching analysis has branched off from Voros McCracken's famous (and controversial) statement, "There is little if any difference among major-league pitchers in their ability to prevent hits on balls hit in the field of play." The research of the analytic community has validated this to some extent, and there are a host of "defense-independent" pitching measures that have been developed to try and extricate the effect of the defense behind a hurler from the pitcher's work.

Our solution to this quandry is Deserved Run Average (DRA), our core pitching metric. DRA looks like earned run average (ERA), the tried-and-true pitching stat you've seen on every baseball broadcast or box score from the past century, but it's very different. To start, DRA takes an event-by-event look at what the pitchers does, and adjusts the value of that event based on different environmental factors like park, batter, catcher, umpire, base-out situation, run differential, inning, defense, home field advantage, pitcher role, and temperature. That mixed model gives us a pitcher's expected contribution, similar to what we do for our DRC+ model for hitters and FRAA model for catchers. (Oh, and we also consider the pitcher's effect on basestealing and on balls getting past the catcher.)

It's important to note that DRA is set to the scale of runs allowed per nine innings (RA9) instead of ERA, which makes DRA's scale slightly higher than ERA's. The reason for this is because ERA tends to overrate three types of pitchers:

1. Pitchers who play in parks where scorers hand out more errors. Official scorers differ significantly in the frequency at which they assign errors to fielders.
2. Ground-ball pitchers, because a substantial proportion of errors occur on grounders.
3. Pitchers who aren't very good. Better pitchers often allow fewer unearned runs than bad pitchers, because good pitchers tend to find ways to get out of jams.

Since the last time you picked up an edition of this book, we've also made a few minor changes to DRA to make it better. Recent research into "tunneling"–the act of throwing consecutive pitches that appear similar from a batter's point of view until after the swing decision point–data has given us a new contextual factor to account for in DRA: plate distance. This refers to the distance between successive pitches as they approach the plate, and while it has a smaller effect than factors like velocity or whiff rate, it still can help explain pitcher strikeout rate in our model.

New Pitching Metrics for 2019

We're including a few "new" pitching metrics for 2019's suite of Baseball Prospectus publications, but you may be familiar with them if you've spent time scouring the internet for stats.

Fastball Percentage

Our fastball percentage (FB%) statistic measures how frequently a pitcher throws a pitch classified as a "fastball," measured as a percentage of overall pitches thrown. We qualify three types of fastballs:

1. The traditional four-seam fastball;
2. The two-seam fastball or sinker;
3. "Hard cutters," which are pitches that have the movement profile of a cut fastball and are used as the pitcher's primary offering or in place of a more traditional fastball.

For example, a pitcher with a FB% of 67 throws any combination of these three pitches about two-thirds of the time.

Whiff Rate

Everybody loves a swing and a miss, and whiff rate (WHF) measures how frequently pitchers induce a swinging strike. To calculate WHF, we add up all the pitches thrown that ended with a swinging strike, then divide that number by a pitcher's total pitches thrown. Most often, high whiff rates correlate with high strikeout rates (and overall effective pitcher performance).

Called Strike Probability

Called Strike Probability (CSP) is a number that represents the likelihood that all of a pitcher's pitches will be called a strike while controlling for location, pitcher and batter handedness, umpire and count. Here's how it works: on each pitch, our model determines how many times (out of 100) that a similar pitch was called for a strike given those factors mentioned above, and when normalized for each batter's strike zone. Then we average the CSP for all pitches thrown by a pitcher in a season, and that gives us the yearly CSP percentage you see in the stats boxes.

As you might imagine, pitchers with a higher CSP are more likely to work in the zone, where pitchers with a lower CSP are likely locating their pitches outside the normal strike zone, for better or for worse.

Projections

Many of you aren't turning to this book just for a look at what a player has done, but for a look at what a player is going to do: the PECOTA projections. PECOTA, initially developed by Nate Silver (who has moved on to greater fame as a political analyst), consists of three parts:

1. Major-league equivalencies, which use minor-league statistics to project how a player will perform in the major leagues;
2. Baseline forecasts, which use weighted averages and regression to the mean to estimate a player's current true talent level; and
3. Aging curves, which uses the career paths of comparable players to estimate how a player's statistics are likely to change over time.

With all those important things covered, let's take a look at what's in the book this year.

Team Prospectus

You bought this book to learn more about your favorite (or maybe least-favorite, who are we to judge?) team, so let's talk about them. After a thoughtful preview of the 2019 season, you'll be presented with our Team Prospectus. This outlines many of the key statistics for each team's 2018 season, as well as a very inviting stadium diagram.

First you'll find the Performance Graphs page. The first is the 2018 Hit List Ranking. This shows our Hit List Rank for the team on each day of the 2018 season and is intended to give you a picture of the ups and downs of the team's season, including their highest and lowest ranks of the year. Hit List Rank measures overall team performance and drives the Hit List Power Rankings at the baseballprospectus.com website.

The second graph is Committed Payroll and helps you see how the team's payroll has compared to the MLB and divisional average payrolls over time. Payroll figures are currents as of January 1, 2019; with so many free agents still unsigned as of this writing, the final 2018 figure will likely be significantly different for many teams. (In the meantime, you can always find the most current data at Baseball Prospectus' Cot's Baseball Contracts page.)

Los Angeles Angels 2019

The third graph is Farm System Ranking and displays how the Baseball Prospectus prospect team has ranked the organization's farm system since 2007. It also indicates the highest and lowest ranks that the farm system achieved over that time.

We start the Team Performance page with the squad's unadjusted and third-order 2018 win-loss records, presented in divisional context. We then list the three highest performing hitters and pitchers by WARP for 2018. Beneath that are a host of other team statistics. **Pythag** presents an adjusted 2018 winning percentage, calculated by taking runs scored per game (**RS/G**) and runs allowed per game (**RA/G**) for the team, and running them through a version of Bill James' Pythagorean formula that was refined and improved by David Smyth and Brandon Heipp. (The formula is called "Pythagenpat," which is equally fun to type and to say.)

Next up is **DRC+**, described earlier, to indicate the overall hitting ability of the team either above or below league-average. Run prevention on the pitching side is covered by **DRA** (also mentioned earlier) and another metric: Fielding Independent Pitching (**FIP**), which calculates another ERA-like statistic based on strikeouts, walks, and home runs recorded. Defensive Efficiency Rating (**DER**) tells us the percentage of balls in play turned into outs for the team, and is a quick fielding shorthand that rounds out run prevention.

After that, we have several measures related to roster composition, as opposed to on-field performance. **B-Age** and **P-Age** tell us the average age of a team's batters and pitchers, respectively. **Salary** is the combined team payroll for all on-field players, and Doug Pappas' Marginal Dollars per Marginal Win (**M$/MW**) tells us how much money a team spent to earn production above replacement level.

Ending this batch of statistics is the number of disabled list days a team had over the season (**DL Days**) and the amount of salary paid to players on the disabled list (**$ on DL**); this final number is expressed as a percentage of total payroll.

Next to each of these stats, we've listed each team's MLB rank in that category from 1st to 30th. In this, 1st always indicates a positive outcome and 30th a negative outcome, except in the case of salary–1st is highest.

The Team Projections page is intended to convey the team's operational capacity entering the 2019 season. We start with the team's PECOTA projected record for 2019, again in divisional context. The **+/-** column indicates how many more or less wins the team is projected to get than they got in 2018. We then list the three highest projected hitters and pitchers by WARP for 2018. A brief farm system summary follows, with the team's top prospect and number of BP Top 101 Prospects. Finally, we list the key new players and departed players, along with their 2019 projected WARP.

Alex Bregman 3B

Born: 03/30/94 Age: 25 Bats: R Throws: R
Height: 6'0" Weight: 180 Origin: Round 1, 2015 Draft (#2 overall)

YEAR	TEAM	LVL	AGE	PA	R	2B	3B	HR	RBI	BB	K	SB	CS	AVG/OBP/SLG
2016	CCH	AA	22	285	54	16	2	14	46	42	26	5	3	.297/.415/.559
2016	FRE	AAA	22	83	17	6	0	6	15	5	12	2	1	.333/.373/.641
2016	HOU	MLB	22	217	31	13	3	8	34	15	52	2	0	.264/.313/.478
2017	HOU	MLB	23	626	88	39	5	19	71	55	97	17	5	.284/.352/.475
2018	HOU	MLB	24	705	105	51	1	31	103	96	85	10	4	.286/.394/.532
2019	*HOU*	*MLB*	*25*	*675*	*96*	*38*	*3*	*23*	*78*	*73*	*107*	*12*	*4*	*.272/.359/.463*

Breakout: 6% Improve: 52% Collapse: 5% Attrition: 2% MLB: 100%
Comparables: Anthony Rendon, David Wright, Pablo Sandoval

YEAR	TEAM	LVL	AGE	PA	DRC+	VORP	BABIP	BRR	FRAA	WARP
2016	CCH	AA	22	285	172	38.9	.286	1.6	SS(51): -3.4, 3B(11): 1.4	2.7
2016	FRE	AAA	22	83	161	10.0	.333	-1.2	SS(14): 2.1, LF(3): -0.1	0.8
2016	HOU	MLB	22	217	107	9.6	.317	0.5	3B(40): 0.9, SS(6): -0.1	1.1
2017	HOU	MLB	23	626	114	34.7	.311	-1.5	3B(132): 8.7, SS(30): -2.9	3.9
2018	HOU	MLB	24	705	150	72.6	.289	-1.6	3B(136): 5.4, SS(28): -0.4	7.4
2019	*HOU*	*MLB*	*25*	*675*	*125*	*37.3*	*.295*	*0.0*	*3B 7, SS 0*	*4.6*

After the projections page, we share a few items about the team's home ballpark. There's the aforementioned diagram of the park's dimensions (including distances to the outfield wall), a few important biographical facts about the stadium, a graphic showing the height of the wall from the left-field pole to the right-field pole, and a table showing three-year park factors for the stadium. The park factors are displayed as indexes where 100 is average, 110 means that the park inflates the statistic in question by 10 percent, and 90 means that the park deflates the statistic in question by 10 percent.

Following the ballpark page, we have a **Personnel** section that lists many of the important decision-makers and upper-level field and operations staff members for the franchise, as well as any former Baseball Prospectus staff members who are currently part of the organization.

Position Players

After all that information and a thoughtful bylined essay covering each team, we present our player comments. Each player is listed with the major-league team who employed him as of early January 2019. If a player changed teams after that point via free agency, trade, or any other method, you'll be able to find them in the book for their previous squad.

First, we cover biographical information (age is as of June 30, 2019) before moving onto the stats themselves. Our statistic columns include standard identifying information like **YEAR**, **TEAM**, **LVL** (level of affiliated play) and **AGE** before getting into the numbers. Next, we provide raw, unstranslated numbers like you might find on the back of your dad's baseball cards: **PA** (plate appearances), **R** (runs), **2B** (doubles), **3B** (triples), **HR** (home runs), **RBI** (runs batted in), **BB** (walks), **K** (strikeouts), **SB** (stolen bases) and **CS** (caught stealing). Then we have unadjusted "slash" statistics: **AVG** (batting average), **OBP** (on-base percentage) and **SLG** (slugging percentage).

Just below the stats box is **PECOTA** data, which is discussed further in a following section. After that, it's on to a pithy and always-informative comment written by a member of the Baseball Prospectus staff, before we cover more stats.

The second text box repeats YEAR, TEAM, LVL, AGE, and PA, then moves on to **DRC+** (Deserved Runs Created Plus), which we described earlier as total offensive expected contribution compared to the league average. Next, one of our oldest active metrics, **VORP** (Value Over Replacement Player), considers offensive production, position and plate appearances. In essence, it is the number of runs contributed beyond what a replacement-level player at the same position would contribute if given the same percentage of team plate appearances. VORP does not consider the quality of a player's defense.

BABIP (batting average on balls in play) tells us how often a ball in play fell for a hit, and can help us identify whether a batter may have been lucky or not … but note that high BABIPs also tend to follow the great hitters of our time, as well as speedy singles hitters who put the ball on the ground.

The next item is **BRR** (Baserunning Runs), which covers all of a player's baserunning accomplishments which includes (but isn't limited to) swiped bags and failed attempts. Next is **FRAA** (Fielding Runs Above Average), which also includes the number of games previously played at each position noted in parentheses. Multi-position players have only their two most frequent positions listed here, but their total FRAA number reflects all positions played.

Our last column here is **WARP** (Wins Above Replacement Player). WARP estimates the total value of a player, which means for hitters it takes into account hitting runs above average (calculated using the DRC+ model), BRR and FRAA. Then, it makes an adjustment for positions played and gives the player a credit for plate appearances based upon the difference between "replacement level"¬–which is derived from the quality of players added to a team's roster after the start of the season¬–and the league average.

Catchers

Catchers are a special breed, and thus they have earned their own separate box which displays some of the defensive metrics that we've built just for them. As an example, let's check out J.T. Realmuto.

YEAR	TEAM	P. COUNT	FRM RUNS	BLK RUNS	THRW RUNS	TOT RUNS
2016	MIA	18935	-8.5	1.8	2.1	-5.6
2017	MIA	18959	5.3	1.7	1.0	9.1
2018	MIA	16399	-0.4	0.9	0.1	0.4
2019	PHI	18448	-1.4	1.5	0.7	0.8

The **YEAR** and **TEAM** columns match what you'd find in the other stat box. **P. COUNT** indicates the number of pitches thrown while the catcher was behind the plate, including swinging strikes, fouls, and balls in play. **FRM RUNS** is the total run value the catcher provided (or cost) his team by influencing the umpire to call strikes where other catchers did not. **BLK RUNS** expresses the total run value above or below average for the catcher's ability to prevent wild pitches and passed balls. **THRW RUNS** is calculated using a similar model as the previous two statistics, and it measures a catcher's ability to throw out basestealers but also to dissuade them from testing his arm in the first place. It takes into account factors like the pitcher (including his delivery and pickoff move) and baserunner (who could be as fast as Billy Hamilton or as slow as Yonder Alonso). **TOT RUNS** is the sum of all of the previous three statistics.

Pitchers

Let's give our pitchers a turn, using 2018 NL Cy Young winner Jacob deGrom as our example. Take a look at his first stat block: the first line and the **YEAR**, **TEAM**, **LVL** and **AGE** columns are the same as in the position player example earlier.

Here too, we have a series of columns that display raw, unadjusted statistics compiled by the pitcher over the course of a season: **W** (wins), **L** (losses), **SV** (saves), **G** (games pitched), **GS** (games started), **IP** (innings pitched), **H** (hits allowed) and **HR** (home runs allowed). Next we have two statistics that are rates: **BB/9** (walks per nine innings) and **K/9** (strikeouts per nine innings), before returning to the unadjusted **K** (strikeouts).

Next up is **GB%** (ground ball percentage), which is the percentage of all batted balls that were hit in the ground, including both outs and hits. Remember, this is based on observational data and subject to human error, so please approach this with a healthy dose of skepticism.

BABIP (batting average on balls in play) is calculated using the same methodology as it is for position players, but it often tells us more about a pitcher than it does a hitter. With pitchers, a high BABIP is often due to poor defense or bad luck, and can often be an indicator of potential rebound, and a low BABIP may be cause to expect performance regression. (A typical league-average BABIP is close to .290-.300.)

After a witty 150ish words on the player like only Baseball Prospectus's staff can provide, it's on to that second stat block, which repeats the YEAR, TEAM, LVL, and AGE columns. The metrics **WHIP** (walks plus hits per inning pitched) and **ERA** (earned run average) are old standbys: WHIP measures walks and hits allowed on a per-inning basis, while ERA measures earned runs on a nine-inning basis. Neither of these stats are translated or adjusted.

DRA (Deserved Run Average) was described at length earlier, and measures how many runs the pitcher "deserved" to allow per nine innings. Please note that since we lack all the data points that would make for a "real" DRA for minor-league events, the DRA displayed for minor league partial-seasons is based off of different data. (That data is a modified version of our cFIP metric, which you can find more information about on our website.)

Jacob deGrom   RHP
Born: 06/19/88   Age: 31   Bats: L   Throws: R
Height: 6'4"   Weight: 180   Origin: Round 9, 2010 Draft (#272 overall)

YEAR	TEAM	LVL	AGE	W	L	SV	G	GS	IP	H	HR	BB/9	K/9	K	GB%	BABIP
2016	NYN	MLB	28	7	8	0	24	24	148	142	15	2.2	8.7	143	47%	.312
2017	NYN	MLB	29	15	10	0	31	31	201^1	180	28	2.6	10.7	239	48%	.305
2018	NYN	MLB	30	10	9	0	32	32	217	152	10	1.9	11.2	269	48%	.281
2019	NYN	MLB	31	13	9	0	31	31	186	145	18	2.3	10.7	221	46%	.286

Breakout: 8%   Improve: 29%   Collapse: 28%   Attrition: 6%   MLB: 85%
Comparables: Erik Bedard, A.J. Burnett, CC Sabathia

YEAR	TEAM	LVL	AGE	WHIP	ERA	DRA	WARP	MPH	FB%	WHF	CSP
2016	NYN	MLB	28	1.20	3.04	3.30	3.5	96.3	59.6	12.1	47.2
2017	NYN	MLB	29	1.19	3.53	3.02	5.7	97.2	55.5	14.5	49.5
2018	NYN	MLB	30	0.91	1.70	2.09	8.0	98.2	52.1	16.3	48.4
2019	NYN	MLB	31	1.02	2.91	3.23	3.9	96.6	54.5	14.8	48.2

Just like with hitters, **WARP** (Wins Above Replacement Player) is a total value metric that puts pitchers of all stripes on the same scale as position players. We use DRA as the primary input for our calculation of WARP. You might notice that relief pitchers (due to their limited innings) may have a lower WARP than you were expecting or than you might see in other WARP-like metrics. WARP does not take leverage into account, just the actions a pitcher performs and the expected value of those actions ... which ends up judging high-leverage relief pitchers differently than you might imagine given their prestige and market value.

MPH gives you the pitcher's 95th percentile velocity for the noted season, in order to give you an idea of what the *peak* fastball velocity a pitcher possesses. Since this comes from our pitch tracking data, it is not publicly available for minor-league pitchers.

Finally, we display the three new pitching metrics we described earlier. **FB%** (fastball percentage) gives you the percentage of fastballs thrown out of all pitches. **WhiffRt** (whiff rate) tells you the percentage of swinging strikes induced out of all pitches. **CS Prob** (called strike probability) expresses the likelihood of all pitches thrown to result in a called strike, after controlling for factors like handedness, umpire, pitch type, count, and location.

PECOTA

All players have PECOTA projections for 2019, as well as a set of other numbers that describe the performance of comparable players according to PECOTA. All projections for 2019 are for the player at the date we went to press in early January and are projected into the league and park context as indicated by the team abbreviation. All PECOTA projected statistics represent a player's projected major-league performance.

The numbers beneath the player's stats–Breakout, Improve, Collapse, Attrition–are part and parcel of the PECOTA projections. They estimate the likelihood of changes in performance relative to the player's previously-established level of production, based on the performance of comparable players:

Breakout Rate is the percent change that a player's production will improve by at least 20 percent relative to the weighted average of his performance over his most recent seasons.

Improve Rate is the percent chance that a player's production will improve at all relative to his baseline performance. A player who is expected to perform just the same as he has in the recent past will have an Improve Rate of 50 percent.

Collapse Rate is the percent chance that a position player's production will decline by at least 25 percent relative to his baseline performance.

Attrition Rate operates on playing time rather than performance. Specifically, it measures the likelihood that a player's playing time will decrease by at least 50 percent relative to his established level.

Breakout Rate and Collapse Rate can sometimes be counterintuitive for players who have already experienced a radical change in performance level. It's also worth noting that the projected decline in a player's rate performances might not be indicative of an expected decline in underlying ability or skill, but could just be an anticipated correction following a breakout season.

MLB% is the percentage of similar players who played in the major leagues in their relevant season.

The final pieces of information are the player's three highest-scoring comparable players as determined by PECOTA. All comparables represent a snapshot of how the listed player was performing at the same age as the current player, so if a 23-year-old pitcher is compared to Bartolo Colon, he's actually being compared to a 23-year-old Colon, not the version that pitched for the Rangers in 2018, nor to Colon's career as a whole.

Los Angeles Angels 2019

A few points about pitcher projections. First, we aren't yet projecting peak velocity, so that column will be blank in the PECOTA lines. Second, projecting DRA is trickier than evaluating past performance, because it is unclear how deserving each pitcher will be of his anticipated outcomes. However, we know that another DRA-related statistic–contextual FIP or cFIP–estimates future run scoring very well. So for PECOTA, the projected DRA figures you see are based on the past cFIPs generated by the pitcher and comparable players over time, along with the other factors described above.

Lineouts

In each chapter's Lineouts section, you'll find abbreviated text comments, as well as most of same information you'd find in our full player comments. We limit the stats boxes in this section to only including the 2018 information for each player.

Exclusive Player Visualizations

In our constant battle to provide you with new and interesting baseball content you can't find anywhere else, we've added a trio of data visualizations to each hitter's entry in these books and a pair of visualizations for each pitcher.

For hitters, you'll find three new infographics. The first is each player's **Batted Ball Distribution**, which displays the five major sections of the field: LF (left), LCF (left center), CF (center), RCF (right center), and RF (right). The percentage indicated tells us what percentage of batted balls from that hitter fell within that part of the field during the 2018 season. We've also included the hitter's slugging percentage on balls in play (also called **SLGCON**) for that part of the field.

You'll also see two heatmaps: **Strike Zone vs LHP** and **Strike Zone vs RHP**. These heat maps represent a view of the strike zone from behind the catcher. Areas where there is a darker coloration represent the places where a higher percentage of pitches resulted in hits. In other words, the heatmap represents a hitter's "sweet spots" for getting hits against either left-handed or right-handed pitchers, depending on the image.

Pitchers get two images that help explain what their pitches look like from a hitter's perspective: **Pitch Shape vs LHH** and **Pitch Shape vs RHH**. These images show you the shape and the "tunneling" effect of each pitcher's offerings from the batter's perspective. For each type of pitch that a pitcher throws (represented by an indicator shape), there's a set of dots indicating the flight path, where each dot represents a 0.01-second interval. This maps the average trajectory and speed of an offering, ending where the ball crosses the plate. The solid black box represents the regular strike zone, while the gray contour lines indicate the range of locations that a pitcher typically works in.

Below the image, we provide a bit more detailed information about each pitcher's average offering in the **Pitch Types** box. Here, we also list each of the pitcher's major offerings under the **Type** column.

- **Fastballs** (which usually refers to the four-seam variation)
- **Sinkers** and/or two-seam fastballs
- **Cutters** (which could include "hard" cutters like cut fastballs and "soft" cutters that resemble hard sliders)
- **Changeups** (not including most splitters)
- **Splitters** (split-fingered pitches, forkballs, and some split-changes)
- **Sliders** and/or slurves
- **Curveballs** (including spike-curveballs and knuckle-curveballs, as well as some slurvy curves)
- **Slow curveballs** and/or eephus pitches
- **Knuckleballs**
- **Screwballs**

The **Freq** column indicates the percentage of overall pitches that fall into each of those type categories; if a pitcher has a 16.55% score for changeups, then that's the percent of all pitches that he throws as changeups. **Velo** is exactly what you think it is: the average miles per hour for each pitch type. **H Mov** is the number of inches of horizontal movement on the average pitch of that type, while **V Mov** is the number of inches of vertical movement on the average pitch of that type. (At Baseball Prospectus, we measure this over the long flight of the ball and include gravity into the V Mov number in order to give you the most realistic representation of what the pitch *actually* does.)

If you're wondering about the second number in brackets, that's the index for that velocity or movement compared to the league average. Like DRC+, a score of 100 means that the speed or movement is about the same as league average, while a higher score means that there's higher velocity or movement than the league average. Numbers below 100 indicate less velocity or movement than the league average.

Part 1: Team Analysis

Table for Two: Previewing the 2019 Los Angeles Angels

Mark Barry and Ginny Searle

GINNY SEARLE: While it may be a more apt metaphor for the A's, it is the Angels who have an elephant in the room. It's now been five years since the Angels and Mike Trout agreed on a six-year, $144.5 million extension, won ninety-eight games, and were swept out of the first round of the playoffs by the Royals. They've yet to return to playoff action, and as next season is Trout's walk (or, ahem, swim) year, it's likely the upcoming winter will be the club's final period of exclusive negotiation with the extra-generational talent. Mark, did the Angels do anything this winter to convince Trout, who despite unfailing politeness has publicly groused about not having a chance to compete in the playoffs, that he should accede to an extension?

MARK BARRY: Well, the Angels signed *some* guys, so I guess sort of? We're in such a weird spot regarding free agency and teams trying to improve, it's hard to say. All of a sudden adding Matt Harvey, Trevor Cahill, Cody Allen, Jonathan Lucroy and Justin Bour on one-year deals is considered a frenetic spending spree. It's sort of the "straddling the fence" strategy they've been trying for the last several seasons; Sign some old guys, hope they're not washed up, move on when they are in fact washed, rinse and repeat. They're probably marginally better, but you bring up a good point. I'm not really sure the team has solidified themselves as perennial contenders to the point where Trout won't look for that life preserver in two years (Get it? Because swimming? From earlier? Ugh, that's so bad… I'm so sorry.)

If you're Mike Trout, a once in an ever player, would you sign an extension in Anaheim? It's not an easy answer, I don't think, especially considering the current landscape.

GINNY: To answer indirectly, the Angels have a plan, or at least purport to. In December GM Billy Eppler explained that he believes "sustainable health is going to be achieved through our farm system," which he intends to shepherd into "top-five" status and bolster via the team's "financial muscle." None of this is revolutionary. It does, however, appear those plans are beginning to materialize. Baseball Prospectus put five Angels prospects on our top 101 list, a figure only seven teams can match. Of the team's top ten prospects, one has debuted, four are expected to this year, and three more (including BP's number two prospect, Jo Adell) are projected to in 2020.

MARK: As an aside—loooooove some Jo Adell. So sorry to interrupt.

GINNY: I'm glad you did—Adell is the Angels' best prospect since Mike Trout, and the cornerstone of a strong system. Beyond security in a barren market, the argument for why Trout would extend his contract (which the team's longest-tenured beat writer considers a likelihood) rests on the organization's ability to show they can consistently compete over the span of his next contract. The catch in that heuristic is that the Angels had a chance to show Trout they were committed to winning this season by making some splashier signings, and instead reached a bevy of one-year commitments. To me, that signifies that the team sees their window as beyond 2019 and is unwilling to pay top dollars for players who are liable to decline by the time the farm supports a competitive team. Maybe I'm putting the cart before the horse here, talking about future seasons, but it feels like Anaheim's front office has figured their ceiling is Wild Card team and decided to work towards building a real championship threat rather than plodding along in half-measures.

MARK: By the way, it seems like "Plodding Along in Half-Measures" might be the league wide motto for the season.

GINNY: Indeed. Given that PECOTA predicts the Halos for their third consecutive 80-win campaign, and the Astros being the Astros, their strategy might not be a bad one. In future years it seems likely the past few seasons will be regarded as a rebuild for the Angels, whose fans were spared the lowest lows due to Mike Trout's transcendence. Still, a team with a player who at 27 is already a Hall of Fame lock, plus Andrelton Simmons and Shohei Ohtani, not to mention the remains of Albert Pujols, Cody Allen, and Matt Harvey, feels like it should be capable of more. Is there anything, or any player, that makes you think the Angels might beat their projections?

MARK: In a lot of ways talking about the future seems like the more important story, or at least the more interesting one for, let's say, 24 teams. It's pretty incredible the way the Angels have turned their system around. After the Simmons trade, their cupboard was pretty bare. As for their big-league club, I agree, I think that there's definitely some room for growth. The 25-man roster isn't exactly littered with plucky, young upstarts, but there are some solid veterans (in addition to the ones you named) like Justin Upton and Kole Calhoun that helped lead the Angels to the 7th best offense last season per DRC+. Fold in Zack Cozart who was really good in 2017, but basically missed all of last season with a balky shoulder, and you have the recipe for another sneaky good offense. Or at least as sneaky of an offense as is possible that includes Mike Trout.

Side note: Do you find yourself calling him Mike Trout, like all the time? I feel like I've almost never gone with just Trout. It's always Mike Trout.

GINNY: Oh, absolutely. He is far too humble to do so, but I wish Mike Trout adopted an illeist affection and began to refer to himself in the third person.

MARK: Anyway, I think the real way for the Angels to beat PECOTA is with a little luck in the health department, specifically in their rotation. Only Andrew Heaney qualified for the ERA title last season (not that his 4.15 ERA was going to be in the running) and only three Angel starters tossed over 100 innings. That's not great. I guess the answer, apparently, was to go and add the aforementioned bastions of health Harvey and Cahill and… oh. At a certain point, you have to think the Angels catch a break with some of these injuries. On the other hand, injured dudes tend to keep getting injured so who knows?

GINNY: You hit the nail on the head. The Angels have built their pitching staffs in recent years from teflon, Big League Chew, and waiver claims, so it is perhaps unsurprising that the team has found itself with a collection of scraps.

MARK: What do you think the chances are that this year is finally the year they get 30 starts from more than one guy (something that hasn't happened since 2015)? And you mentioned the burgeoning farm system, do you think there's any short-term help on the way on that front?

GINNY: As to the new additions, the Dark Knight actually topped thirty starts for the first time last season, but I wouldn't take the over on him repeating. Cahill, meanwhile, hasn't started more than twenty games since 2013. So if the Angels are going to have two pitchers crest thirty starts, the most realistic candidates are Tyler Skaggs, Andrew Heaney, and Jaime Barria. Heaney putting up something resembling his 3.5 WARP over 180 innings last year (contrasted with his 0.9 WARP projection) seems almost a prerequisite for the Angels securing a Wild Card berth. Skaggs, meanwhile, produced well enough over 125 1/3 innings to remind fans that he's a former blue-chip prospect, but he has never started more than twenty-eight combined games in a season at any level. Finally, PECOTA simply does not think Barria, projected for 0.2 WARP in 111 innings, is very good.

MARK: I agree that Skaggs could be one of the answers here. He was really good in the first half, with a 2.56 ERA and striking out over a batter per inning over 98 frames. The second half? You guessed it. Injured. But still, finishing with a 3.86 DRA and 129 punch outs in those 125 1/3 innings, while staying under three walks per nine? That's promising.

GINNY: Skaggs certainly has the most upside of anyone currently in the rotation; it wasn't just because both he and Patrick Corbin were included in the 2010 Dan Haren trade that comparisons have been drawn between the southpaws. In terms of depth, PECOTA projects both Griffin Canning, the team's number two prospect, and Taylor Cole, whom the club signed on a minor-league contract last spring, to be better by DRA than the entire rotation. Cole was solid over 36 big league innings, if not as solid as his 2.75 ERA implies. Canning appears to be basically ready, but the Angels will presumably give the twenty-two year old time in Triple-A to build on his 59 innings there (and conveniently miss the Super Two cutoff).

On the whole, the Angels' pitching corps could be better than it appears. Their bullpen, too, has a new look, and while it thinks Allen's decline will continue, PECOTA believes in Ty Buttrey and Justin Anderson. It does not think as highly of fellow flamethrowers (and righties—this team has one left-handed reliever) Luis Garcia, Hansel Robles, and the injured Keynan Middleton, but the team nevertheless will have one of the league's highest-octane relief units with serious breakout potential.

The problem with the Angels' pitching projections is how much they would have to surpass them by to contend: no team projected for 85+ wins has more than 700 runs against, and the Angels are projected for 795. Do you think this pitching staff could surprise us enough, Mark? Or that the team's hitting could be strong enough to offset it?

MARK: So, I kinda/sorta liked the way the Angels built their rotation, but I'm too superstitious to say it out loud. After hashing it out a bit in this conversation, I do think they might surprise some folks. There's not really an ace on the staff, but there are at least four solid number three starters, and that's not counting the inevitable arrival of Canning to round out the rotation. As an aside, maybe this is the time to talk about how I miss watching Ohtani pitch.

GINNY: We saw exactly one Ohtani start where he had all of his pitches working, and he ran a perfect game into the seventh. So I commiserate.

MARK: Nevertheless, I don't think they really need dominance from their rotation, they need volume. There's enough talent there to keep their heads above water, as long as they don't have to rely on guys in the mold of Odrisamer Despaigne and Deck McGuire to make consistent starts. I'm getting a little more excited about their prospects, and that's coming from someone who picked them to win a Wild Card last year.

GINNY: There's definitely upside here if the pitching impresses.

I want to mention two infielders, David Fletcher and Luis Rengifo. Fletcher broke out in a massive way offensively last season in Triple-A (.955 OPS), and FRAA thought so highly of his defense he was worth 1.6 WARP in his first 80 big league games. Rengifo, too, impressed with his bat: the Angels' return for C.J. Cron blitzed through three levels and recorded a 112 DRC+ in a taste of Triple-A. Do you think we may have missed any other potential breakouts?

MARK: Those are both good ones. You mentioned Fletcher's first taste of big-league reps last season, and I think Rengifo could follow a similar trajectory. Flashing a really nice approach at the dish and plenty of flexibility defensively. Both could be mix-and-match infielders this season, which would immensely help an otherwise older team.

Ok, so this might be crazy, and I know the answer is very probably "no" for lots of reasons, but is there a chance we see Adell this season? He struggled a bit in a short Double-A stint to close out 2018, but if he comes back and mashes in Mobile… maybe? As a comparison, Mike Trout got his first call up to the big leagues in 2011, straight from Double-A, after slashing .326/.414/.544 in 412 plate appearances. Adell hit .290/.345/.546 at High-A Inland Empire this season. It's not exactly apples to apples, but I'm just saying…

GINNY: It's possible, particularly if Calhoun's bat looks like it did in the first half last season; given how granularly teams monitor service time these days, though, I doubt we see Adell for long, if at all. The Angels have little in the way of outfield depth, however, and if a stopgap is needed Adell, at nineteen, would likely be a bigger help than, say, Jared Walsh, no matter how compelling it is that Walsh reported as a two-way player.

MARK: Should we do a few quick hits before getting outta here?

Which number do you project to be higher? Mike Trout WARP or nights Matt Harvey is spotted at a Hollywood club the night before a start?

GINNY: Especially as Harvey is already injured with a glute strain, I have to go with Mike Trout.

Last year, Andrelton Simmons had his first season being rated by FRAA as a below-average defensive shortstop; do you think he returns to +5.0 FRAA or more this season (a figure he reached every year of his career until 2018)?

MARK: That's really surprising, wow. He'll spend almost all of the 2019 season as a 29-year-old, so he's still young-ish. I'll say he bounces back to be the defensive wizard we all know and love.

How about a few predictions? Ginny, the million-dollar question. What do you think the Angels' record will be in 2019, and will it be good enough to sneak a Wild Card spot?

GINNY: I think the Halos will have surprises in store this year; I see them beating their projection and winning 85. In a still-stratified AL, though, I just don't see that getting them to the playoffs. What about you, Mark?

MARK: I really want to see Mike Trout in the playoffs. And I do agree with you that I'm a little more optimistic about their season than PECOTA seems to be. That said, the A's had to win 97 games last season to get the second Wild Card. That's crazy. The Angels could have a 2018 Mariners season, win 89 games, and still be like 10 games out. It's kind of a bummer. But for the sake of thoroughness, let's say 86-76, while falling out of the race when summer turns to fall.

GINNY: Hey, if the Angels stay in the race until after the trade deadline, at least we can avoid months of hearing Eppler and new Angels manager Brad Ausmus (got it in under the wire) peppered with questions of whether they will trade Mike Trout. That's something, right?

Right?

Performance Graphs

2018 Hit List Ranking

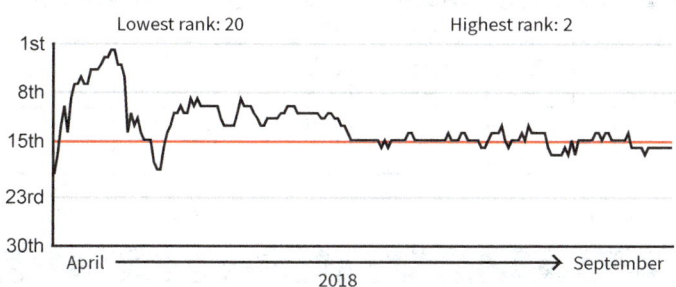

Committed Payroll (in millions)

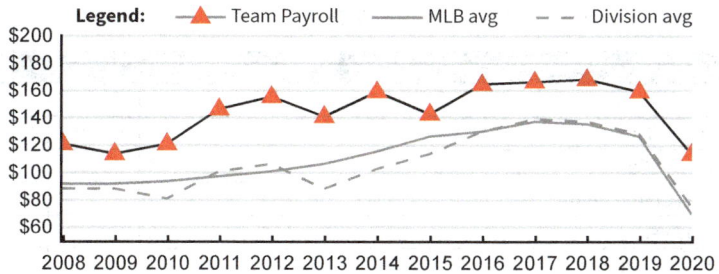

Farm System Ranking

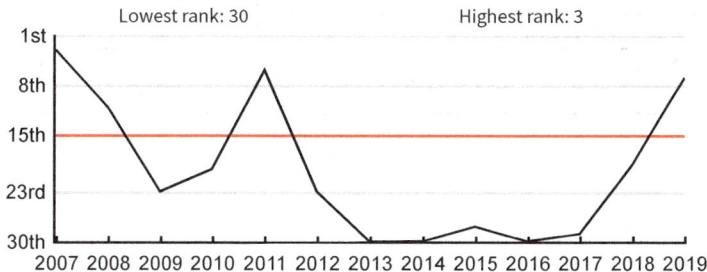

2018 Team Performance

ACTUAL STANDINGS

Team	W	L	Pct
HOU	103	59	.635
OAK	97	65	.598
SEA	89	73	.549
ANA	**80**	**82**	**.493**
TEX	67	95	.413

THIRD-ORDER STANDINGS

Team	W	L	Pct
HOU	108	54	.666
OAK	96	66	.592
SEA	82	80	.506
ANA	**80**	**82**	**.493**
TEX	68	94	.419

TOP HITTERS

Player	WARP
Mike Trout	8.2
Justin Upton	4.4
Andrelton Simmons	2.9

TOP PITCHERS

Player	WARP
Andrew Heaney	3.5
Shohei Ohtani	2.8
Tyler Skaggs	2.1

VITAL STATISTICS

Statistic Name	Value	Rank
Pythagenpat	.499	15th
Runs Scored per Game	4.45	15th
Runs Allowed per Game	4.46	18th
Deserved Runs Created Plus	102	7th
Deserved Run Average	4.60	21st
Fielding Independent Pitching	4.39	21st
Defensive Efficiency Rating	.706	15th
Batter Age	29.6	28th
Pitcher Age	27.3	8th
Salary	$166.7M	6th
Marginal $ per Marginal Win	$4.9M	9th
Disabled List Days	$1,622.0M	29th
$ on DL	19%	20th

2019 Team Projections

PROJECTED STANDINGS

Team	W	L	Pct	+/-
HOU	98	64	.604	-5
ANA	**80**	**82**	**.493**	**0**
OAK	79	83	.487	-18
TEX	71	91	.438	+4
SEA	70	92	.432	-19

TOP PROJECTED HITTERS

Player	WARP
Mike Trout	8.4
Justin Upton	4.2
Andrelton Simmons	3.1

TOP PROJECTED PITCHERS

Player	WARP
Tyler Skaggs	2.1
Shohei Ohtani	2
Trevor Cahill	1.3

FARM SYSTEM REPORT

Top Prospect	Number of Top 101 Prospects
Jo Adell, #2	5

KEY DEDUCTIONS

Player	WARP
Matt Shoemaker	1.2
Garrett Richards	1.1
Blake Parker	0.4

KEY ADDITIONS

Player	WARP
Trevor Cahill	1.3
Justin Bour	0.9
Matt Harvey	0.7
Cody Allen	0.4
Luis Garcia	0.4

Team Personnel

President
John Carpino

General Manager
Billy Eppler

Assistant General Manager
Steve Martone

Assistant General Manager
Jonathan Strangio

Manager
Brad Ausmus

Angel Stadium Stats

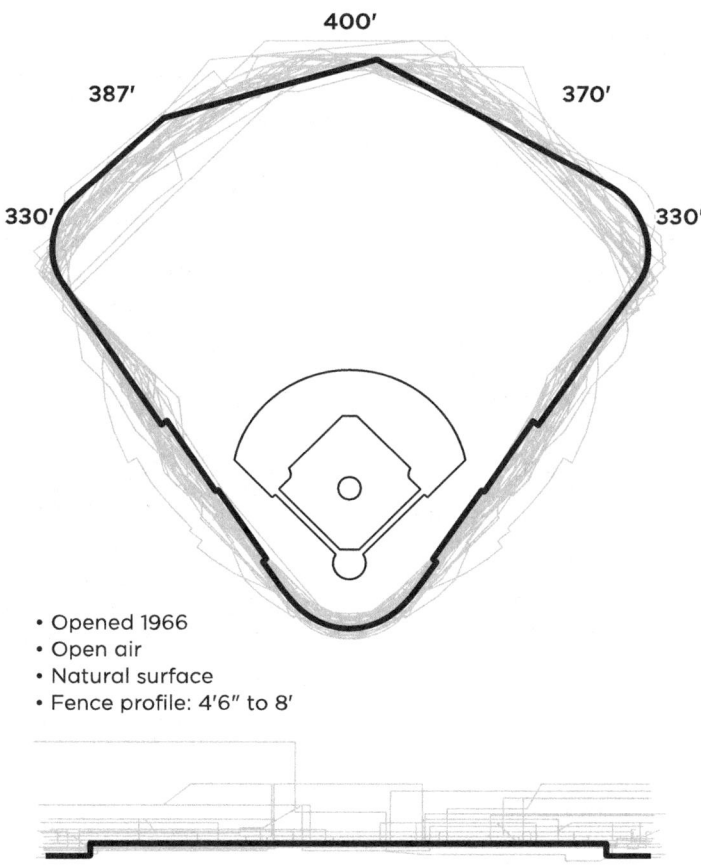

- Opened 1966
- Open air
- Natural surface
- Fence profile: 4'6" to 8'

Three-Year Park Factors

Runs	Runs/RH	Runs/LH	HR/RH	HR/LH
98	97	99	103	104

Angels Team Analysis

On April 3rd, Shohei Ohtani came to the plate for the Angels in the bottom of the first. There were two out. The bases were loaded. Mike Trout had already homered in the inning, turning what had been a 2-0 lead for Cleveland into a 2-1 lead; a Kole Calhoun RBI single brought the score to a 2-2 tie, where it stood as Ohtani walked slowly to the plate. It was his first home plate appearance as a major league baseball player. The fans packing Angels Stadium rose to their feet; the crush of photographers and reporters who had come from far and wide specifically to document this moment stood at attention. And around the world, the signal went out, through texts and tweets and push notifications. If you were a baseball fan—no matter which team you rooted for, no matter which continent you lived on—this was the moment you were paying attention to. It was April, and the center of the baseball universe was in Anaheim.

The first pitch from Cleveland's Josh Tomlin was a ball outside. The second was a cutter, down and in; Ohtani fouled it off. He swung over a low curveball. The count stood at 1-2; the crowd was a tremor of anxious anticipation. Tomlin's fourth pitch to Ohtani almost hit him. It rolled past Roberto Perez, allowing Calhoun to score from third. 3-2 Angels. Ohtani's first home plate appearance could no longer end in a grand slam.

And you began to feel a little foolish for expecting, even a little bit, that this plate appearance was ever really going to end in a grand slam. You try to inculcate yourself against such romantic high hopes in baseball. The perfect outcome is so rare. And for Ohtani to succeed—for Ohtani to succeed in this moment, in this way—would be too perfect of an outcome to hope for. You were warned when he decided to play in the major leagues, and you were warned when he signed with the Angels, donned that too-bright red jersey, and you were warned when spring training rolled around and the reports began to flow in. Don't hype the guy up so much. He was no Babe Ruth. There were injury concerns. The stuff was there, but not polished enough. The swing was too easily exploited. He would never hit in the major leagues. As Ohtani fouled off another pitch, still with two strikes on him, you tempered your hope, and with you, so did everyone else watching, the millions of eyes all turned to this one man, hoping.

And then Tomlin threw a curveball down and in. A swing, a crack, the voice of the stadium rising. The ball arcing high into the air—is it gone? is it really gone?—coming down in the uplifted arms of some random, grinning fan. Ohtani rounded the bases, face serious, a hand on his helmet, holding it in place. When he reached the dugout, he took his helmet off and broke into a smile. His teammates gave him the silent treatment for as long as they could bear it. Then they converged upon him.

⚾   ⚾   ⚾

We all read the same baseball news at the end of the day, the big, important stories that have national columns written about them. We read analysis of specific player performances that we may not necessarily have seen ourselves, follow up on our fantasy rosters. But for the majority of people with a strong interest in baseball, whether they're fans or beat writers, that interest is filtered through one team, maybe two. Baseball is, after all, so vast. There are just so many teams, and so many games, and within those games dozens of batted ball events, hundreds of pitches. It's much easier to process that amount of information through the convenient narrative arc of a single team's season. It's a way of making it all make sense.

With the number of teams in baseball, and the number of games that each of those teams play, though, this means the collective consciousness of the baseball-watching public is largely fragmented. A hypothetical someone who is an exclusive devotee of the San Diego Padres, for example, might have very little overlap between the content of their baseball consumption and that of a die-hard Red Sox fan. The moments that make up the story of their respective seasons, the sounds and images of their day-to-day baseball interactions, will be almost completely different from each other. A large part of the appeal of the postseason, then, is the fact that it represents a convergence of all these perspectives. From the alternating chaos and numbness of September comes an expectant silence, a baseball-universal waiting for a single event. All the narratives flow into one; all of the disparate perspectives unite. Everyone is hanging on the same pitches, breathing in the same pauses, waiting for the narrative of the season to write its ending.

Moments like these are rare in the regular season. They often center around some historic milestone. Everyone will tune in when a pitcher is three outs away from a perfect game, or when a player is one home run away from an all-time landmark, but these kinds of universal must-watch events are few and far between. And for the Los Angeles Angels of the last decade, they have been almost non-existent. Yes, the Angels have had Mike Trout, who might end up being the best player ever. Trout's greatness, though, is a cumulative, consistent greatness. Trout's greatness is not composed of the kinds of distinct events around which the world of baseball can turn. You could make an argument for Trout being must-watch television whenever he takes the field, but the team around him as a whole has been undeniably uncompelling.

Even the Angels' one postseason appearance in the last years—a 98-win division-title campaign in 2014—was unmemorable at best. The Angels were swept by the wild-card Kansas City Royals. They scored six runs in three games. Since that season, the Angels have been on the losing end of mediocre, plagued by inconsistent pitching, even less consistent hitting, an apparently unfillable void in left field, and the ongoing burden of Albert Pujols' overwhelming contract and overwhelming age.

Billy Eppler's tenure as general manager has seen the improvement of a farm system bereft of talent to one featuring several top-end prospects, leaving it ranked somewhere in the middle of the road in terms of MLB-wide rankings. But a Jo Adell doesn't currently translate to an interesting Major League team; his Venn Diagram and Trout's may hardly overlap. The Angels have failed to bring one of the greatest players of all time anywhere close to a championship. And with the arrival of the dominant Astros, they have become not only an afterthought in their geographic area—the Dodgers, a team that already possessed of a pervasive cultural cachet that has eluded the Angels, have won six straight division titles—but an afterthought in the division as well. With three years of Mike Trout left, the Angels' best offseason efforts could only reasonably put them in contention for the second Wild Card spot alongside a slough of other not-great teams.

In 2018, though, they had Shohei Ohtani, by far the offseason's biggest topic of conversation. They added Zack Cozart and Ian Kinsler to shore up their infield. And for two weeks in April, the Angels were the undeniable center of the baseball universe. They were now not simply the team wasting Mike Trout's talent, but the team with Mike Trout and Shohei Ohtani. The Angels went 13-3 in their first 16 games, their best start to a season in franchise history. Trout had his first-ever 0-for-6 game on Opening Day and went through a 1-for-18 stretch, yet his line was still Troutian in its quality. Cozart performed well at the plate, while shoring up the left side of the Angels' infield. Andrelton Simmons continued to be Andrelton Simmons.

The contributions were far-ranging, but every conversation about the Angels' success ended up being about Ohtani. After that first homer, he hit two more homers in his next two games. In his first start, he pitched six innings, allowing three runs on a home run and striking out six. His next start—his first home start—was incredible. He cut through the Oakland A's lineup, a lineup that would end the year as one of baseball's best offenses, striking out 12 over seven scoreless innings. Through the first six of those, he was perfect.

⚾   ⚾   ⚾

Much is made of the grind of a 162-game season, the burden it puts on a player's mind and body. Significant injuries are a part of any team's journey from March to September, and the teams that survive are often the ones who have the good fortune and depth enough that the injuries don't become the story of the season. The Angels' injuries started early, and they didn't stop. First came Ian Kinsler, one of their key offseason acquisitions, who got a left adductor strain sliding into second on March 31st. Pitcher JC Ramirez went down with UCL damage on April 17th. Closer Keynan Middleton went down with the same injury on May 22nd, and so did reliever Blake Wood on May 30th. Most devastating of all was the UCL damage Ohtani suffered, taking him out of the rotation from early June onward — and as if that weren't enough, Garrett Richards, too, fell to Tommy John in mid-July. The Angels' rotation had already appeared to be a weakness of the team. That rotation itself being utterly and completely decimated by injury made it untenable.

And though the Angels' position players were less severely affected, they were far from immune. Kole Calhoun—who had to that point been posting historically terrible numbers at the plate—was placed on the DL in late May. Andrelton Simmons was sidelined with an ankle sprain in early June. Zack Cozart dislocated his shoulder—also in early June.

On Monday, May 15th, the Angels remained tied with the Mariners for the lead in the AL West. A month later, that tie had turned into a 7 1/2 game deficit.

⚾ ⚾ ⚾

The signal went out again on September 2nd. By this point, the Angels' postseason hopes had long since evaporated: They were four games under .500, 18 games back in the division. It had been months since they had played any baseball one might consider "meaningful"; they'd been sellers at the deadline, trading away catcher Martin Maldonado and the recently-acquired Kinsler. But as the Angels took the field in Houston, facing the Astros team that had so far lapped them in the division, the eyes of the baseball-watching public turned en masse once again in expectation of a Shohei Ohtani start. There was anticipation, but anticipation not of the stunning perfection that had seemed possible and then become fulfilled back in April. This time, the anticipation was tinged with anxiety. Ohtani was making his return to the mound. The range of realistic good options were somewhat limited. The range of realistic disasters was massive. For Ohtani to be pitching at all in September was far sooner than most had expected. The baseball-watching public was united not in hope, but in anxiety.

Ohtani's first pitch to George Springer came in at 96.9 mph—a fastball outside for ball one. His second, another fastball at 95.7, was poked into right field for a base hit. Ohtani got out of the inning without allowing a run to score. But the second inning was more concerning. His average fastball velocity fell from 97.4 mph in the first to 95.5 in the second. In the third, it fell all the way to 91.4 mph; he recorded one out, gave up a two-run homer to Springer, and was pulled from the game.

Both the Angels and Ohtani insisted that his elbow was fine. It wasn't. On September 30th, Ohtani underwent Tommy John surgery.

At season's end, Mike Scioscia announced his departure from the role of manager, after over two decades at the helm of the team—one of baseball's most distinctive figures finally ousted from his position, replaced by a non-descript Brad Ausmus. Because while this team has grown accustomed to losing over the last decade, 2018 was a different kind of loss. The world saw, for a few weeks, what this team could be when everything was going right, before everything went back to being wrong.

The Angels only have Mike Trout for a few more years. They won't have Shohei Ohtani the two-way player back for a while. In a division with the Astros, and now with the A's, the chances of them reaching anything close to the heights of competition in the foreseeable future are slim. But it is not even the dim hopes for a competitive team that constitutes the great disappointment of the 2018 Angels. For a few weeks at the beginning of the season, the Angels were the center of the baseball universe. For a few weeks, they were a manifestation of the wildest hopes and dreams any baseball fan could have coming true. There was Mike Trout, and there was a fully-realized Shohei Ohtani, playing on the same nearly-unbeatable team. The outcome, in the end, remained the same. They became another team struggling with injury, another losing team in the American League. Another losing season in Anaheim. The promise of the 2018 Angels faded once again into the expected outcomes of an uninteresting team, the afterthought of the AL West, too far removed from the glow of Hollywood's lights to catch any of their shine. The great disappointment is that the Angels couldn't hold that perfect moment together. They might not have another one any time soon.

—*Rachael McDaniel is an author of Baseball Prospectus.*

Part 2: Player Analysis

Los Angeles Angels 2019

Justin Bour 1B

Born: 05/28/88   Age: 31   Bats: L   Throws: R
Height: 6'3"   Weight: 265   Origin: Round 25, 2009 Draft (#770 overall)

YEAR	TEAM	LVL	AGE	PA	R	2B	3B	HR	RBI	BB	K	SB	CS	AVG/OBP/SLG
2016	MIA	MLB	28	321	35	12	1	15	51	38	56	0	0	.264/.349/.475
2017	MIA	MLB	29	429	52	18	0	25	83	47	95	1	0	.289/.366/.536
2018	MIA	MLB	30	447	43	10	1	19	54	69	111	1	0	.227/.347/.412
2018	PHI	MLB	30	54	6	3	0	1	5	4	13	1	0	.224/.296/.347
2019	ANA	MLB	31	396	52	17	1	18	57	42	84	1	0	.269/.348/.477

Breakout: 1%   Improve: 36%   Collapse: 15%   Attrition: 9%   MLB: 85%
Comparables: Allen Craig, Justin Smoak, Jesus Guzman

First basemen are weird, man. One year, you're OPSing .900 and swatting some megaton bombs in your home park during the Home Run Derby, the next your slugging percentage is 120 points in the red and you're getting traded within the division for a single prospect not even on a Top 20 list. So goes the saga of Justin Bour, whom the Phillies picked up to provide pure offensive depth and who…did not quite provide pure offensive depth. Hampered by an oblique injury and a depth chart already crammed with corner players, Bour made just 54 trips to the plate with his new team and did little to reverse what had already been, to that point, a disappointing season. After Philadelphia predictably cut ties the Angels swooped in to beef up a first base/designated hitter depth chart sagging under the weight of the back end of Pujols' contract. Bour should get some chances to reignite the stick while Ohtani mends, but his cheap contract and ever-present platoon issues signal a limited engagement if he starts slow.

YEAR	TEAM	LVL	AGE	PA	DRC+	VORP	BABIP	BRR	FRAA	WARP
2016	MIA	MLB	28	321	119	17.7	.278	-1.1	1B(82): -5.1	0.5
2017	MIA	MLB	29	429	126	30.2	.322	-1.8	1B(102): -10.0	0.8
2018	MIA	MLB	30	447	103	14.3	.267	-3.1	1B(103): -6.3	-0.2
2018	PHI	MLB	30	54	103	-0.9	.286	0.2	1B(10): -0.5	0.1
2019	ANA	MLB	31	396	119	15.8	.302	-0.6	1B -8	0.9

Justin Bour, continued

Batted Ball Distribution

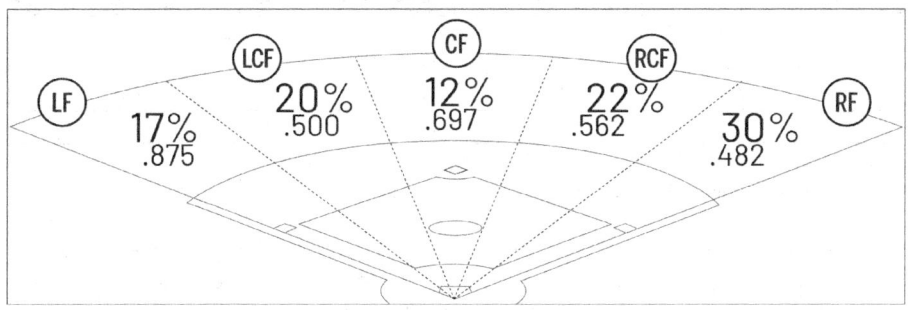

Strike Zone vs LHP

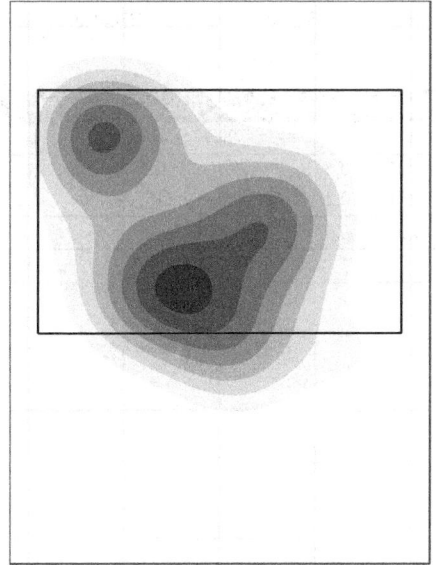

Strike Zone vs RHP

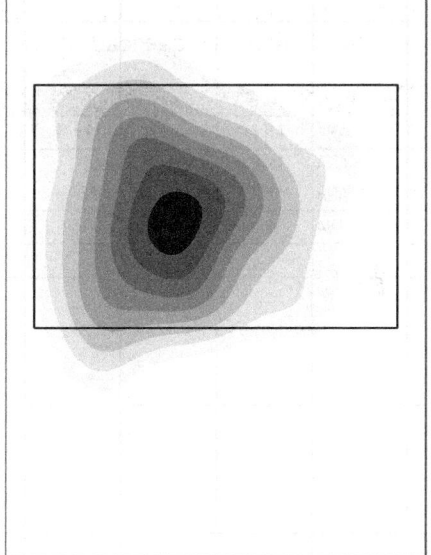

Kole Calhoun RF

Born: 10/14/87 Age: 31 Bats: L Throws: L
Height: 5'10" Weight: 200 Origin: Round 8, 2010 Draft (#264 overall)

YEAR	TEAM	LVL	AGE	PA	R	2B	3B	HR	RBI	BB	K	SB	CS	AVG/OBP/SLG
2016	ANA	MLB	28	672	91	35	5	18	75	67	118	2	3	.271/.348/.438
2017	ANA	MLB	29	654	77	23	2	19	71	71	134	5	1	.244/.333/.392
2018	ANA	MLB	30	552	71	18	2	19	57	53	133	6	2	.208/.283/.369
2019	ANA	MLB	31	656	84	30	2	19	68	65	135	5	2	.250/.331/.408

Breakout: 4% Improve: 33% Collapse: 13% Attrition: 18% MLB: 91%
Comparables: Curt Walker, Johnny Callison, Nate Schierholtz

Calhoun had one of the worst months of May since Anne Boleyn's arrest and execution, spilling out a .314 OPS in considerable playing time. (The last time someone had a monthly OPS that low with 20 starts was 11 years ago.) He emerged from a brief DL stint with a brand new crouched stance, and the adjustment paid off big-time, as he rode significantly more aerial contact to an OPS nearly four times higher in July. So don't let the season stats fool you too much: He still has plenty of range in right field and is a strong candidate to return to a league-average leadoff hitter.

YEAR	TEAM	LVL	AGE	PA	DRC+	VORP	BABIP	BRR	FRAA	WARP
2016	ANA	MLB	28	672	113	23.5	.309	0.1	RF(154): -6.7	1.8
2017	ANA	MLB	29	654	99	10.9	.284	-0.6	RF(154): 10.0	2.3
2018	ANA	MLB	30	552	85	-3.1	.241	-0.2	RF(136): -3.7, CF(4): -0.2	-0.2
2019	ANA	MLB	31	656	104	22.5	.294	-0.6	RF -2, CF 0	1.8

Kole Calhoun, continued

Batted Ball Distribution

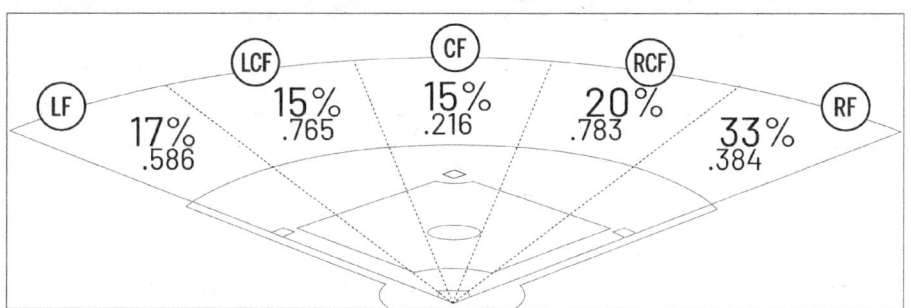

Strike Zone vs LHP

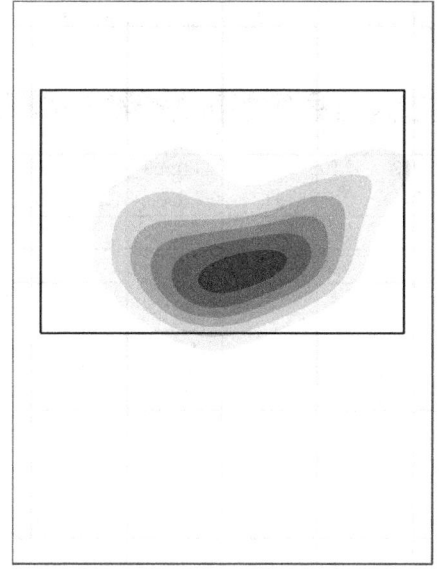

Strike Zone vs RHP

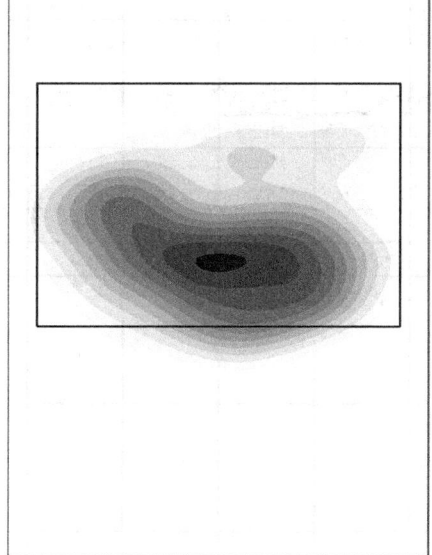

Angels Player Analysis - 25

Zack Cozart   INF

Born: 08/12/85   Age: 33   Bats: R   Throws: R
Height: 6'0"   Weight: 205   Origin: Round 2, 2007 Draft (#79 overall)

YEAR	TEAM	LVL	AGE	PA	R	2B	3B	HR	RBI	BB	K	SB	CS	AVG/OBP/SLG
2016	CIN	MLB	30	508	67	28	2	16	50	37	84	4	1	.252/.308/.425
2017	CIN	MLB	31	507	80	24	7	24	63	62	78	3	0	.297/.385/.548
2018	ANA	MLB	32	253	29	13	2	5	18	19	42	0	0	.219/.296/.362
2019	ANA	MLB	33	452	54	22	3	14	54	44	77	2	1	.263/.340/.439

Breakout: 0%   Improve: 32%   Collapse: 18%   Attrition: 14%   MLB: 90%
Comparables: Pie Traynor, George Kell, Martin Prado

Cozart broke out in 2017 and then broke in the more traditional sense last year amidst an ocean of change: new team, new league, new time zone, new position. He also missed half the year to shoulder surgery. He was probably never a 138 DRC+ guy to begin with, but moving around the diamond seemed difficult for him, or so the defensive metrics tell us. If healthy he should still be able to crank out enough extra-base hits to steady the bottom-third of a lineup, and two years of eight guaranteed figures apiece will certainly give Anaheim plenty of incentive to let him try.

YEAR	TEAM	LVL	AGE	PA	DRC+	VORP	BABIP	BRR	FRAA	WARP
2016	CIN	MLB	30	508	93	20.4	.274	3.1	SS(111): 2.6	2.4
2017	CIN	MLB	31	507	137	51.2	.312	-2.8	SS(112): 1.3	4.5
2018	ANA	MLB	32	253	90	3.5	.244	-0.2	3B(35): -0.7, 2B(16): -0.2	0.5
2019	ANA	MLB	33	452	109	16.9	.288	-0.3	3B -6, 2B 0	0.9

Zack Cozart, continued

Batted Ball Distribution

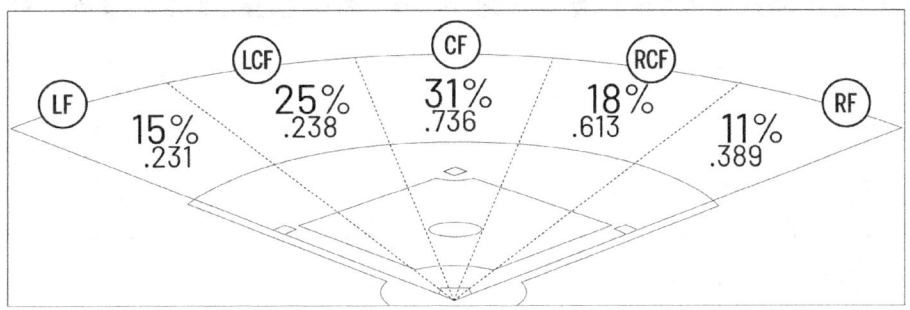

Strike Zone vs LHP   **Strike Zone vs RHP**

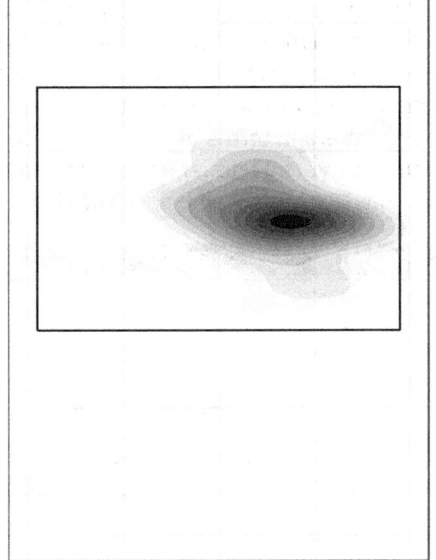

David Fletcher INF

Born: 05/31/94 Age: 25 Bats: R Throws: R
Height: 5'10" Weight: 175 Origin: Round 6, 2015 Draft (#195 overall)

YEAR	TEAM	LVL	AGE	PA	R	2B	3B	HR	RBI	BB	K	SB	CS	AVG/OBP/SLG
2016	INL	A+	22	355	42	12	1	3	31	22	43	15	3	.275/.321/.346
2016	ARK	AA	22	83	10	6	0	0	6	3	13	1	0	.300/.325/.375
2017	MOB	AA	23	272	32	14	1	1	22	21	30	12	5	.276/.341/.354
2017	SLC	AAA	23	217	27	6	1	2	17	6	25	8	1	.254/.285/.322
2018	SLC	AAA	24	275	55	25	5	6	37	16	21	7	2	.350/.394/.559
2018	ANA	MLB	24	307	35	18	2	1	25	15	34	3	0	.275/.316/.363
2019	ANA	MLB	25	499	57	19	3	10	44	26	69	9	2	.248/.295/.367

Breakout: 12% Improve: 54% Collapse: 2% Attrition: 37% MLB: 65%
Comparables: Kevin Frandsen, Tyler Pastornicky, Donovan Solano

It's impossible to hear about Fletcher without someone invoking another David: Eckstein. The latter also came up with the Angels with a papier-mache bat and the ability to play all over the infield. There are a few differences, of course. Eckstein was a true shortstop for the early part of his career, lessening the demand on his offense. Fletcher also struck out more in his inaugural 80 games than Eckstein ever did over the course of an entire season. Fletcher needs that kind of regular contact to get balls through the infield and get on base. It's a different era in terms of strikeouts, but it's also an era where teams carry fewer bench players. Fletcher has the tool set to be an end-of-the-bench guy—we'll just have to find out if he's in the right time period.

YEAR	TEAM	LVL	AGE	PA	DRC+	VORP	BABIP	BRR	FRAA	WARP
2016	INL	A+	22	355	98	11.7	.307	1.6	SS(47): -6.2, 2B(28): -0.2	-0.1
2016	ARK	AA	22	83	107	5.0	.358	0.6	SS(18): 2.3	0.5
2017	MOB	AA	23	272	113	10.1	.308	-1.5	2B(34): 1.0, SS(28): 0.0	0.7
2017	SLC	AAA	23	217	59	-0.1	.281	2.3	SS(26): 0.2, 2B(22): 0.2	-0.1
2018	SLC	AAA	24	275	138	24.4	.364	3.4	SS(31): 3.4, 2B(18): -1.6	2.6
2018	ANA	MLB	24	307	91	6.6	.307	3.5	2B(43): 1.8, 3B(33): 4.7	1.6
2019	ANA	MLB	25	499	79	7.6	.267	0.7	2B -1, SS 0	0.4

David Fletcher, continued

Batted Ball Distribution

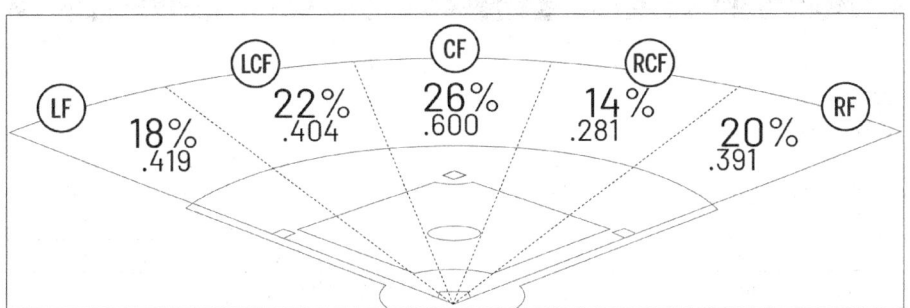

Strike Zone vs LHP

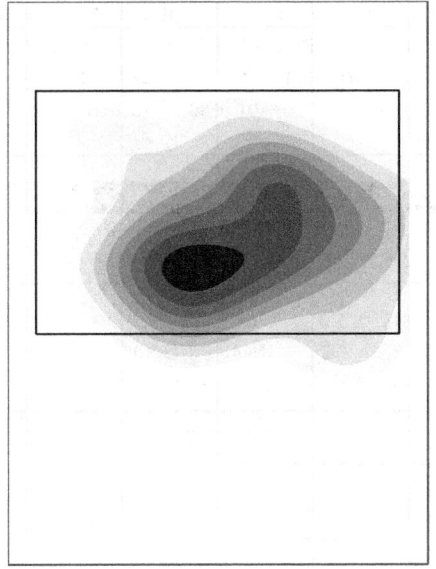

Strike Zone vs RHP

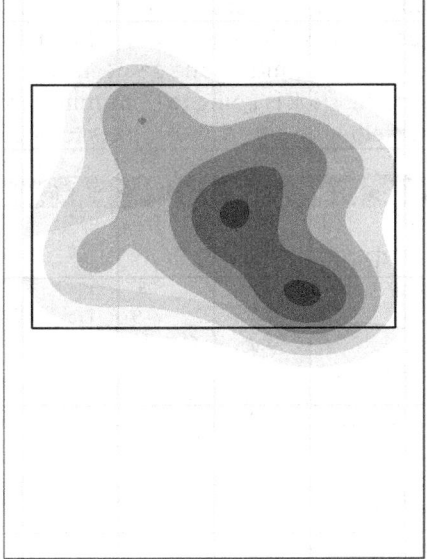

Michael Hermosillo OF

Born: 01/17/95 Age: 24 Bats: R Throws: R
Height: 5'11" Weight: 190 Origin: Round 28, 2013 Draft (#847 overall)

YEAR	TEAM	LVL	AGE	PA	R	2B	3B	HR	RBI	BB	K	SB	CS	AVG/OBP/SLG
2016	BUR	A	21	160	22	8	1	2	22	18	22	4	3	.326/.411/.442
2016	INL	A+	21	174	36	7	4	4	17	16	30	6	7	.309/.393/.490
2017	INL	A+	22	64	5	6	0	0	2	9	15	5	2	.321/.438/.434
2017	MOB	AA	22	340	40	13	2	4	26	40	73	21	9	.248/.361/.353
2017	SLC	AAA	22	129	20	6	1	5	16	7	28	9	2	.287/.341/.487
2018	SLC	AAA	23	323	43	14	4	12	46	30	87	10	5	.267/.357/.480
2018	ANA	MLB	23	62	7	4	0	1	1	3	17	0	1	.211/.274/.333
2019	ANA	MLB	24	232	28	7	1	7	24	19	66	7	3	.206/.287/.353

Breakout: 11% Improve: 33% Collapse: 4% Attrition: 19% MLB: 49%
Comparables: Brian Goodwin, Brandon Nimmo, Brian Anderson

Just by making his debut, Hermosillo more than justified the 28th-round pick the Angels spent on him in 2013. The former three-star University of Illinois football recruit doesn't lack for athleticism, and showed it of at all three outfield positions. He doubled for his first major-league hit, but was never able to string together two hits in one game. It was a small sample, to be sure, but his ability with the stick is going to determine whether he's more—or less—than the fourth outfielder he currently projects to become.

YEAR	TEAM	LVL	AGE	PA	DRC+	VORP	BABIP	BRR	FRAA	WARP
2016	BUR	A	21	160	151	10.4	.377	0.2	CF(20): -4.9, LF(11): -0.6	0.4
2016	INL	A+	21	174	149	22.5	.359	2.5	CF(25): -3.3, RF(8): -0.7	0.6
2017	INL	A+	22	64	161	4.2	.447	-1.3	CF(9): -2.3, LF(3): -0.3	0.0
2017	MOB	AA	22	340	116	15.4	.316	-2.0	CF(52): -2.3, RF(13): 2.3	0.7
2017	SLC	AAA	22	129	90	5.3	.337	0.3	LF(14): -0.1, CF(10): 0.6	0.2
2018	SLC	AAA	23	323	90	11.6	.341	-0.4	CF(36): 5.5, RF(19): 0.3	1.0
2018	ANA	MLB	23	62	61	-1.2	.282	-0.5	CF(12): 1.5, RF(12): 0.7	0.1
2019	ANA	MLB	24	232	75	1.1	.260	0.2	CF -1, LF -1	0.0

Michael Hermosillo, continued

Batted Ball Distribution

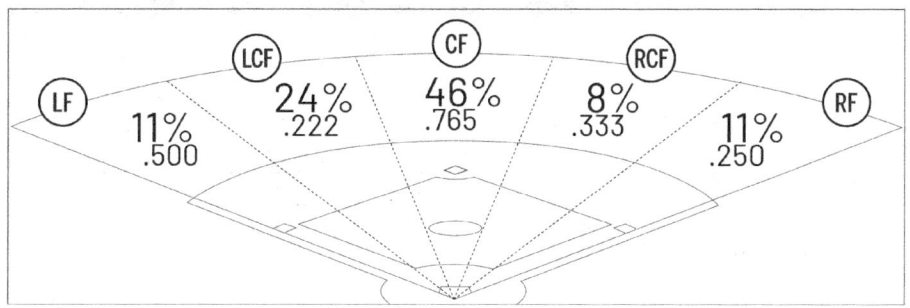

Strike Zone vs LHP   Strike Zone vs RHP

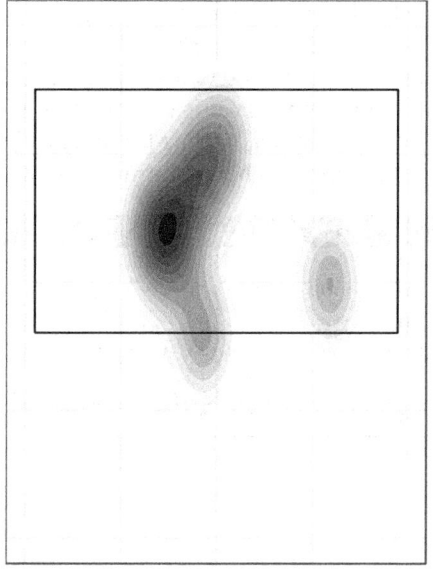

Tommy La Stella 2B

Born: 01/31/89   Age: 30   Bats: L   Throws: R
Height: 5'11"   Weight: 180   Origin: Round 8, 2011 Draft (#266 overall)

YEAR	TEAM	LVL	AGE	PA	R	2B	3B	HR	RBI	BB	K	SB	CS	AVG/OBP/SLG
2016	IOW	AAA	27	46	6	2	0	1	3	2	9	0	0	.273/.304/.386
2016	CHN	MLB	27	169	17	12	1	2	11	18	27	0	1	.270/.357/.405
2017	IOW	AAA	28	121	14	2	0	1	6	10	22	0	1	.218/.281/.264
2017	CHN	MLB	28	151	18	8	0	5	22	20	18	0	0	.288/.389/.472
2018	CHN	MLB	29	192	23	8	0	1	19	17	27	0	1	.266/.340/.331
2019	ANA	MLB	30	354	37	15	1	8	36	30	66	1	1	.248/.319/.377

Breakout: 0%   Improve: 38%   Collapse: 14%   Attrition: 17%   MLB: 82%
Comparables: Jeff Keppinger, Luis Rodriguez, Eric Sogard

After refusing an assignment to Triple-A in mid-2016 because he wanted to play only in Chicago, La Stella eventually got what he wanted: he was ever-present on the Cubs roster, appearing in over 75 percent of the team's games. At the same time, he was as peripheral as ever, starting just 24 times and seeing PH next to his name so often he might as well have been followed around by a GIF of Eleanor Shellstrop shouting "Ya Basic" at him. He hit well enough off the bench, though, and while the glove is more passable than remarkable at second and third, there's value in embodying replacement level. The Angels clearly think so, anyway, trading for him in a lo-fi deal that should provide him with a shot at reprising his performance in 2019.

YEAR	TEAM	LVL	AGE	PA	DRC+	VORP	BABIP	BRR	FRAA	WARP
2016	IOW	AAA	27	46	83	-0.2	.324	0.4	3B(6): 0.9, 2B(4): -0.6	0.0
2016	CHN	MLB	27	169	97	8.0	.319	-1.8	3B(33): -3.3, 2B(9): -0.9	-0.1
2017	IOW	AAA	28	121	53	-3.6	.261	1.0	2B(22): 0.3, 3B(4): 0.0	-0.3
2017	CHN	MLB	28	151	114	11.6	.298	-0.7	2B(21): -2.4, 3B(18): -0.5	0.4
2018	CHN	MLB	29	192	84	3.0	.312	0.7	3B(26): -1.8, 2B(15): 0.3	0.2
2019	ANA	MLB	30	354	86	4.7	.286	-0.8	2B -2, 3B -3	-0.2

Tommy La Stella, continued

Batted Ball Distribution

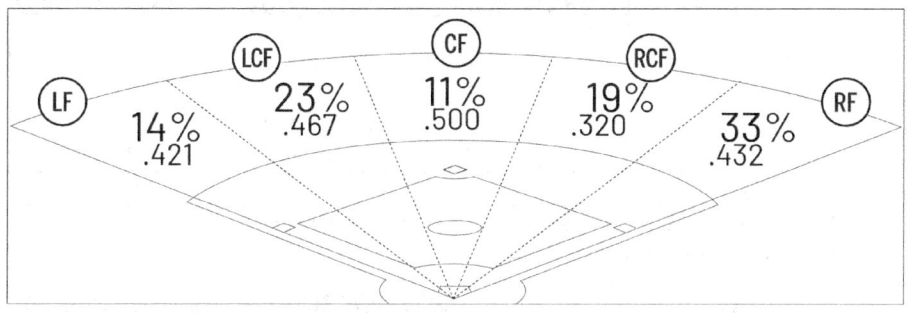

Strike Zone vs LHP　　　　　**Strike Zone vs RHP**

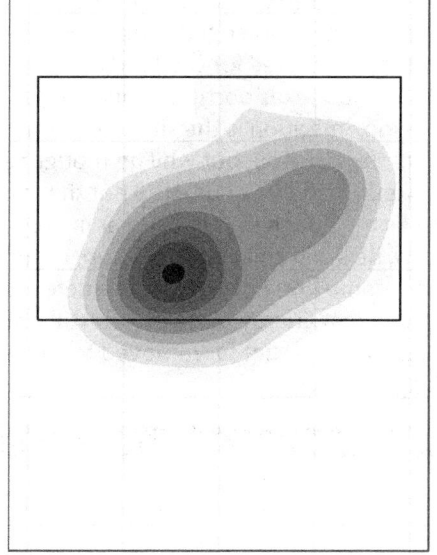

Angels Player Analysis - 33

Jonathan Lucroy C

Born: 06/13/86 Age: 33 Bats: R Throws: R
Height: 6'0" Weight: 200 Origin: Round 3, 2007 Draft (#101 overall)

YEAR	TEAM	LVL	AGE	PA	R	2B	3B	HR	RBI	BB	K	SB	CS	AVG/OBP/SLG
2016	MIL	MLB	30	376	48	17	3	13	50	33	70	5	0	.299/.359/.482
2016	TEX	MLB	30	168	19	7	0	11	31	14	30	0	0	.276/.345/.539
2017	TEX	MLB	31	306	27	15	0	4	27	19	32	1	0	.242/.297/.338
2017	COL	MLB	31	175	18	6	3	2	13	27	19	0	0	.310/.429/.437
2018	OAK	MLB	32	454	41	21	1	4	51	29	65	0	0	.241/.291/.325
2019	ANA	MLB	33	396	42	18	2	8	40	35	62	1	0	.257/.328/.387

Breakout: 5% Improve: 32% Collapse: 18% Attrition: 15% MLB: 93%
Comparables: Del Crandall, Hank Severeid, Paul Lo Duca

Lucroy signed a very late free-agent deal with the A's for less money (just $6.5 million) than you might expect after he averaged about 2.7 WARP over the prior three years. Sometimes, though, the market gets it right, as Lucroy replicated for Oakland the disastrous Texas portion of his 2017 season. Imitation is the sincerest form

YEAR	TEAM	P. COUNT	FRM RUNS	BLK RUNS	THRW RUNS	TOT RUNS
2016	MIL	11622	3.8	2.1	2.2	7.5
2016	TEX	5788	1.8	-0.2	2.2	3.5
2017	TEX	9640	-11.1	-1.2	0.6	-12.2
2017	COL	5958	-6.8	-1.8	0.1	-8.8
2018	OAK	16900	-3.7	-3.7	0.3	-7.3
2019	ANA	14396	-7.9	-1.4	1.0	-8.4

of flattery and all, but why he thought a replacement-level season needed flattering is beyond us. He's not the framer he once was behind the plate, and he lacks the punch to put any fear into opposing pitchers. Even if this is what he is now, he's still a playable backup, especially if you want him to do a Yoda routine with some hotshot youngster's defense, and there's always the chance that this is *not* what Lucroy is, since he's still only 33 (despite a very respectable amount of grizzle) and not far removed from being one of the better catchers in the league.

YEAR	TEAM	LVL	AGE	PA	DRC+	VORP	BABIP	BRR	FRAA	WARP
2016	MIL	MLB	30	376	120	32.1	.340	2.0	C(82): -1.2, 1B(6): -0.6	2.7
2016	TEX	MLB	30	168	125	12.8	.279	-1.1	C(44): -0.4	1.2
2017	TEX	MLB	31	306	95	0.0	.259	1.0	C(66): -0.7, 1B(1): 0.0	1.2
2017	COL	MLB	31	175	93	13.8	.341	-0.2	C(44): 0.6	0.8
2018	OAK	MLB	32	454	82	2.4	.273	-2.5	C(125): -9.7	0.0
2019	ANA	MLB	33	396	91	14.2	.285	-0.4	C -11	0.1

Jonathan Lucroy, continued

Batted Ball Distribution

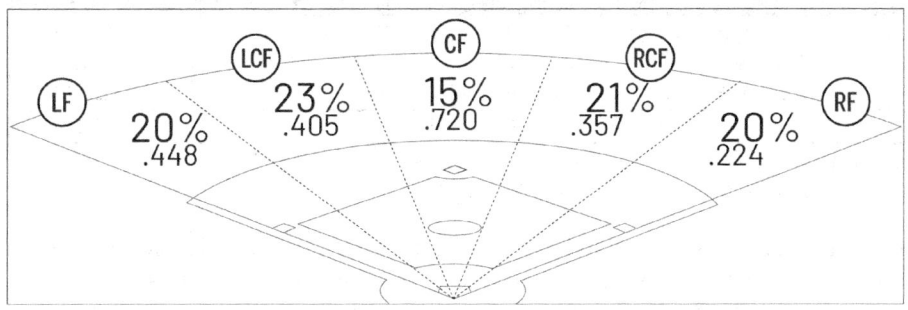

Strike Zone vs LHP

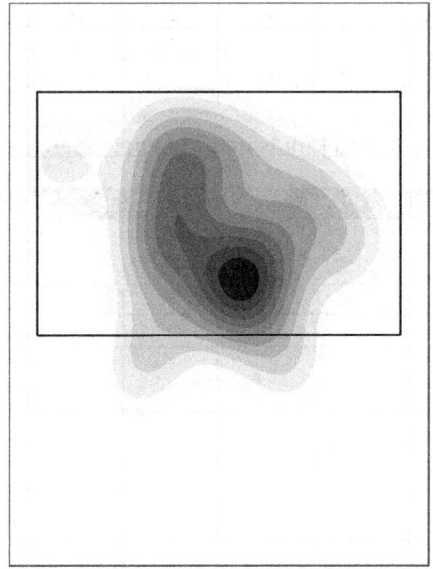

Strike Zone vs RHP

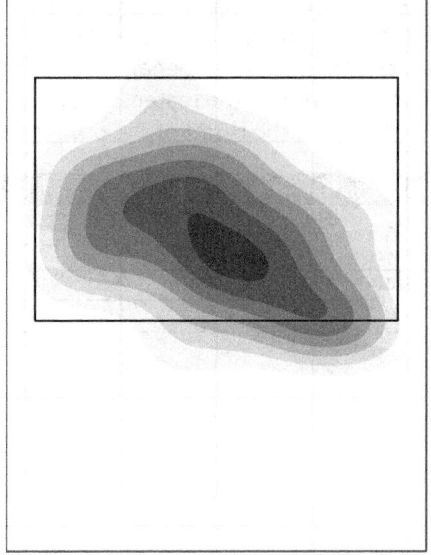

Albert Pujols 1B

Born: 01/16/80 Age: 39 Bats: R Throws: R
Height: 6'3" Weight: 240 Origin: Round 13, 1999 Draft (#402 overall)

YEAR	TEAM	LVL	AGE	PA	R	2B	3B	HR	RBI	BB	K	SB	CS	AVG/OBP/SLG
2016	ANA	MLB	36	650	71	19	0	31	119	49	75	4	0	.268/.323/.457
2017	ANA	MLB	37	636	53	17	0	23	101	37	93	3	0	.241/.286/.386
2018	ANA	MLB	38	498	50	20	0	19	64	28	65	1	0	.245/.289/.411
2019	ANA	MLB	39	496	54	20	1	15	59	39	72	2	0	.251/.312/.399

Breakout: 0% Improve: 10% Collapse: 29% Attrition: 13% MLB: 71%
Comparables: Victor Martinez, Eddie Murray, Hideki Matsui

In Milton's epic poem *Paradise Lost*, we learn about the band of angels who rebelled against God, ultimately lost and were banished to Hell. Their leader, Satan, began to plot their revenge by tempting Adam and Eve into the most forbidden of fruits: a long-term contract for Pujols. They were warned of the grave consequences. Of course they shouldn't have done this, but mind you this poem takes place years ago, when we were all a bit naive. Eve, excited to get a Hall of Famer in his prime, signed Pujols to a 700-year contract. Adam was not without sin either, as he agreed to a full no-trade clause. The angels decided to honor the contract as penance for Adam and Eve's recklessness, and to this day Pujols still roams the roster and gets plenty of plate appearances. Satan, however, got the brunt of the punishment: he had Pujols in his keeper league.

YEAR	TEAM	LVL	AGE	PA	DRC+	VORP	BABIP	BRR	FRAA	WARP
2016	ANA	MLB	36	650	119	11.8	.260	-3.8	1B(28): -1.1	1.8
2017	ANA	MLB	37	636	90	-17.7	.249	-1.2	1B(6): -0.6	-0.1
2018	ANA	MLB	38	498	101	1.2	.247	-1.9	1B(70): 3.8	1.0
2019	ANA	MLB	39	496	96	4.7	.269	-0.6	1B 1	0.7

Albert Pujols, continued

Batted Ball Distribution

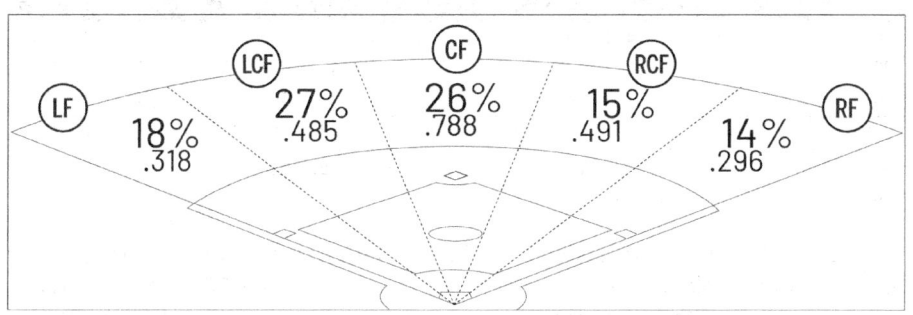

Strike Zone vs LHP   **Strike Zone vs RHP**

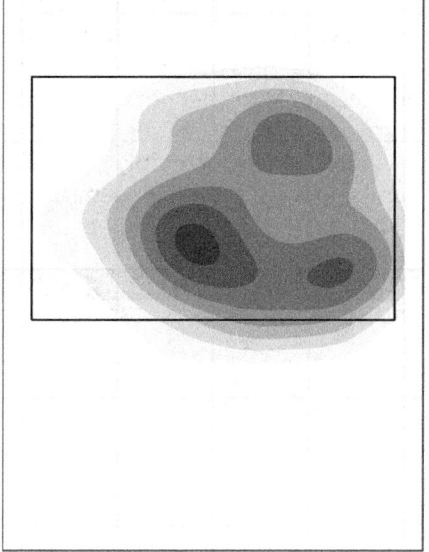

Andrelton Simmons SS

Born: 09/04/89 Age: 29 Bats: R Throws: R
Height: 6'2" Weight: 200 Origin: Round 2, 2010 Draft (#70 overall)

YEAR	TEAM	LVL	AGE	PA	R	2B	3B	HR	RBI	BB	K	SB	CS	AVG/OBP/SLG
2016	ANA	MLB	26	483	48	22	2	4	44	28	38	10	1	.281/.324/.366
2017	ANA	MLB	27	647	77	38	2	14	69	47	67	19	6	.278/.331/.421
2018	ANA	MLB	28	600	68	26	5	11	75	35	44	10	2	.292/.337/.417
2019	ANA	MLB	29	584	66	28	4	12	63	47	61	12	3	.278/.341/.415

Breakout: 1% Improve: 46% Collapse: 5% Attrition: 7% MLB: 96%
Comparables: Elvis Andrus, Gil Garrido, Nellie Fox

Simmons has won six straight Fielding Bible awards, most in that award's history, and he's played six-and-a-half seasons. His negative FRAA last year is a shocking outlier, but its explanation is a bit inside baseball, so ... oh, right, this is a baseball book. Essentially, the grounder rates for the Angels were very consistent year-to-year, and Simmons just made considerably fewer overall plays in 2018, namely assists, than one would estimate. That dinged the numbers, but feel free to chalk it up to single-season defensive metric wackiness. He remained tops in shortstop Defensive Runs Saved, putouts and double plays. He's the best active defensive shortstop and remains highly durable. And to further not compare him with Ozzie Smith, Simmons has improved as a hitter, setting career bests in average and on-base percentage, while maintaining incredibly good contact rates. He still has never been named to an All-Star team, but he seems to be finally entering his prime, as if ground-ball hitters needed to hear that.

YEAR	TEAM	LVL	AGE	PA	DRC+	VORP	BABIP	BRR	FRAA	WARP
2016	ANA	MLB	26	483	94	15.3	.298	0.8	SS(124): 6.2	2.5
2017	ANA	MLB	27	647	102	31.8	.291	2.7	SS(158): 16.1	5.0
2018	ANA	MLB	28	600	107	35.6	.300	3.8	SS(145): -6.8	2.9
2019	ANA	MLB	29	584	107	30.8	.292	0.8	SS 2	3.1

Andrelton Simmons, continued

Batted Ball Distribution

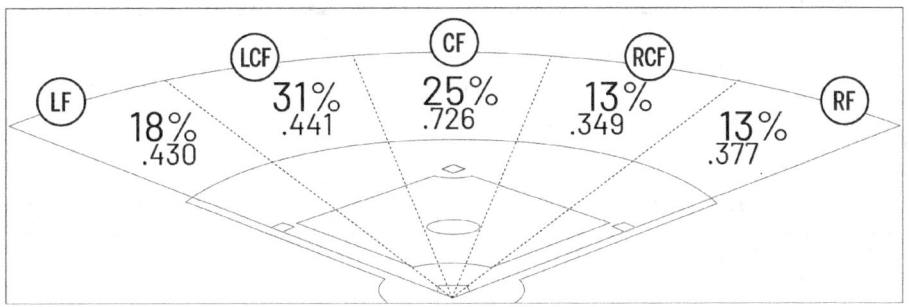

Strike Zone vs LHP

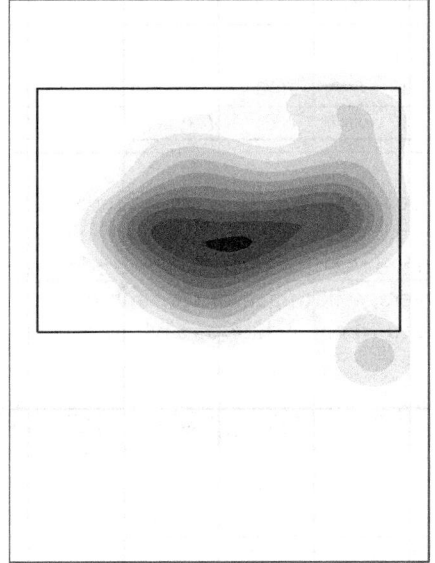

Strike Zone vs RHP

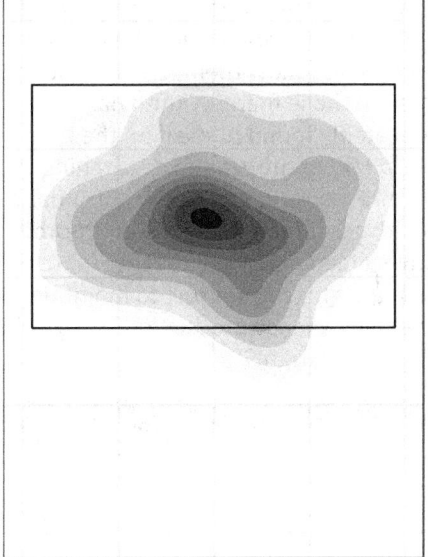

Kevan Smith C

Born: 06/28/88   Age: 31   Bats: R   Throws: R
Height: 6'4"   Weight: 230   Origin: Round 7, 2011 Draft (#231 overall)

YEAR	TEAM	LVL	AGE	PA	R	2B	3B	HR	RBI	BB	K	SB	CS	AVG/OBP/SLG
2016	CHR	AAA	28	205	18	9	0	8	24	16	36	0	0	.219/.291/.399
2016	CHA	MLB	28	16	2	0	0	0	0	0	6	0	0	.125/.125/.125
2017	CHR	AAA	29	62	10	6	0	0	15	6	9	0	0	.377/.435/.491
2017	CHA	MLB	29	294	23	17	0	4	30	9	46	0	0	.283/.309/.388
2018	CHR	AAA	30	124	12	4	0	4	16	8	18	0	0	.268/.331/.411
2018	CHA	MLB	30	187	21	6	0	3	21	10	18	1	0	.292/.348/.380
2019	ANA	MLB	31	162	16	6	0	4	16	10	29	0	0	.223/.280/.345

Breakout: 5%   Improve: 33%   Collapse: 10%   Attrition: 18%   MLB: 82%
Comparables: Brayan Pena, Steve Clevenger, Manny Pina

Some inquisitive souls in Los Angeles finally grew curious on how sustainable Smith's above-average on-base percentage and average framing would be in a larger role. They would be right to follow their curiosity, since despite those merits, Smith has repeatedly found himself on the periphery of the White Sox catching picture, backing up the likes of Omar Narvaez. Give him credit for his tenacity: Smith continued to toil at self-improvement at an age when his bosses might have already given up looking for it. He'll need to continue to defy the odds as he enters his thirties just to maintain his average-hitting, average-running, average-defense production. But you've seen what catchers as a whole hit like these days, right?

YEAR	TEAM	P. COUNT	FRM RUNS	BLK RUNS	THRW RUNS	TOT RUNS
2016	CHA	396	-0.2	0.2	0.0	-0.2
2017	CHA	10862	1.6	-1.6	-3.9	-4.5
2017	CHR	1944	0.1	-0.4	-0.1	-0.4
2018	CHA	6961	1.5	-0.9	-0.3	0.7
2018	CHR	2973	0.4	-0.8	-0.2	-0.5
2019	ANA	6306	-0.3	-1.0	-0.6	-1.9

YEAR	TEAM	LVL	AGE	PA	DRC+	VORP	BABIP	BRR	FRAA	WARP
2016	CHR	AAA	28	205	80	-0.2	.229	-1.1	C(43): -2.1	-0.2
2016	CHA	MLB	28	16	68	-1.0	.200	0.7	C(6): -0.1	0.1
2017	CHR	AAA	29	62	161	5.5	.435	0.5	C(13): -0.2	0.6
2017	CHA	MLB	29	294	80	6.4	.323	0.5	C(79): -6.2	0.1
2018	CHR	AAA	30	124	103	2.6	.286	-1.0	C(22): -0.7	0.2
2018	CHA	MLB	30	187	101	7.4	.311	0.2	C(47): 0.1	1.0
2019	ANA	MLB	31	162	76	3.3	.257	-0.3	C -3	-0.1

Kevan Smith, continued

Batted Ball Distribution

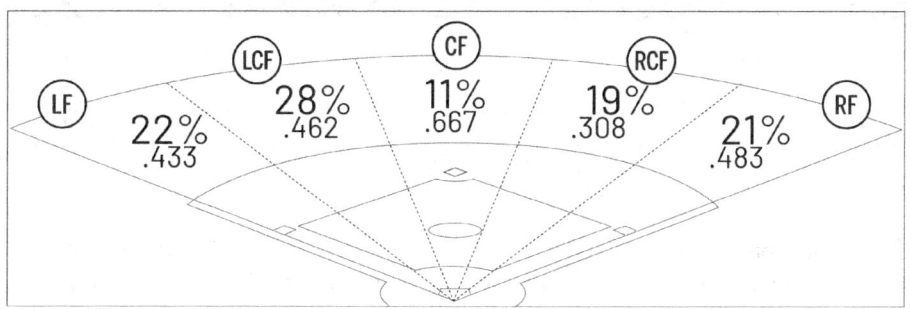

Strike Zone vs LHP

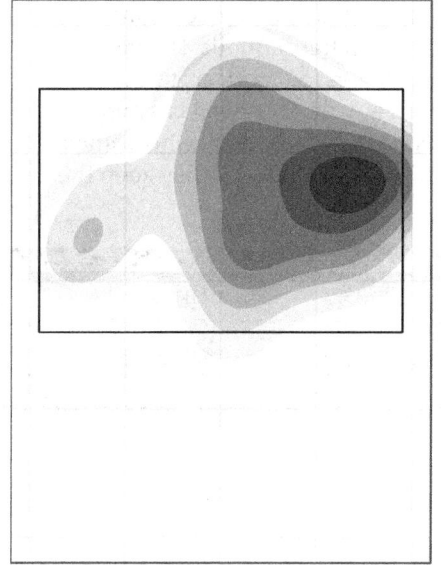

Strike Zone vs RHP

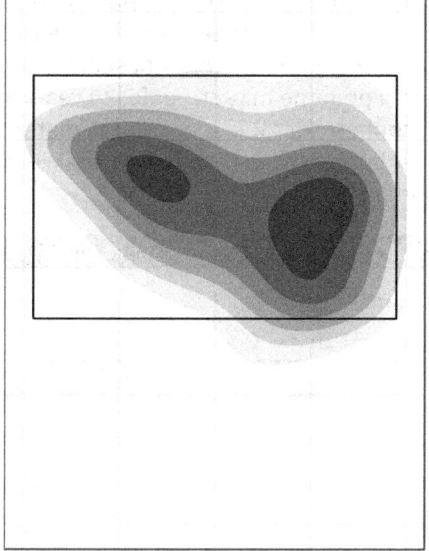

Mike Trout CF

Born: 08/07/91 Age: 27 Bats: R Throws: R
Height: 6'2" Weight: 235 Origin: Round 1, 2009 Draft (#25 overall)

YEAR	TEAM	LVL	AGE	PA	R	2B	3B	HR	RBI	BB	K	SB	CS	AVG/OBP/SLG
2016	ANA	MLB	24	681	123	32	5	29	100	116	137	30	7	.315/.441/.550
2017	ANA	MLB	25	507	92	25	3	33	72	94	90	22	4	.306/.442/.629
2018	ANA	MLB	26	608	101	24	4	39	79	122	124	24	2	.312/.460/.628
2019	ANA	MLB	27	674	127	31	4	34	100	138	131	27	5	.305/.455/.575

Breakout: 1%   Improve: 49%   Collapse: 9%   Attrition: 1%   MLB: 98%
Comparables: Joe Dimaggio, Mickey Mantle, Frank Thomas

Part of baseball's generational allure is the day-to-day grind, the struggle to persist in the face of adversity and how it relates to a fan's personal journey. Trout has faced adversity but he still hasn't struggled. This past year he achieved the Jay Jaffe JAWS threshold for a Hall of Fame center fielder, as if you were yet convinced, and is younger than 15 rookies who had 100 plate appearances in 2018, including Joey Wendle and Luke Voit and Nick Martini. He has struggled only to struggle. We can't relate, we can only venerate. He is the diamond standard, already standing alone with ghosts and Barry Bonds. He once again set a career high in OPS—baseball's best single-season mark since Bonds. At some point he may struggle, 30 years from now, when baseball is a mindless cacophony of robots, all modeled after this baseball player, all who dominate baseball yet keep short-circuiting when it rains. Which is why they keep the human Trout employed.

YEAR	TEAM	LVL	AGE	PA	DRC+	VORP	BABIP	BRR	FRAA	WARP
2016	ANA	MLB	24	681	166	90.7	.371	4.8	CF(148): -6.8	7.6
2017	ANA	MLB	25	507	176	69.0	.318	0.0	CF(108): -3.3	6.2
2018	ANA	MLB	26	608	183	92.0	.346	1.5	CF(125): -2.5	8.2
2019	ANA	MLB	27	674	177	90.8	.343	2.8	CF -9	8.4

Mike Trout, continued

Batted Ball Distribution

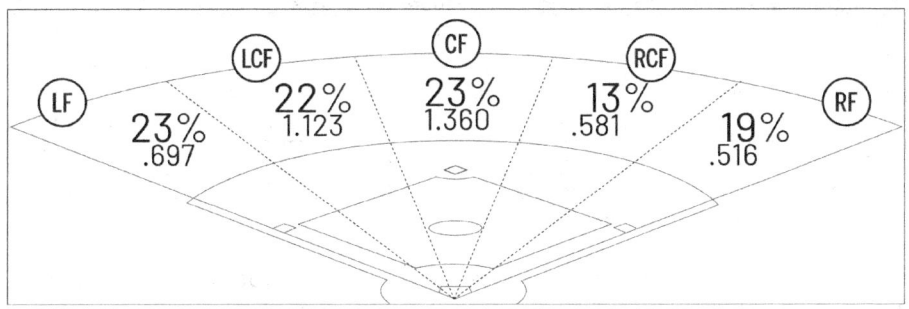

Strike Zone vs LHP   **Strike Zone vs RHP**

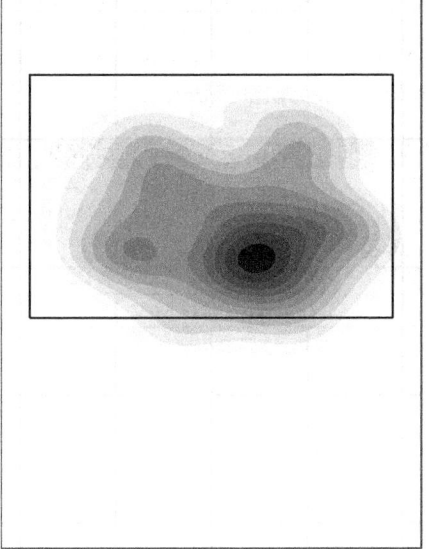

Angels Player Analysis - 43

Justin Upton LF

Born: 08/25/87   Age: 31   Bats: R   Throws: R
Height: 6'2"   Weight: 205   Origin: Round 1, 2005 Draft (#1 overall)

YEAR	TEAM	LVL	AGE	PA	R	2B	3B	HR	RBI	BB	K	SB	CS	AVG/OBP/SLG
2016	DET	MLB	28	626	81	28	2	31	87	50	179	9	4	.246/.310/.465
2017	DET	MLB	29	520	81	37	0	28	94	57	147	10	5	.279/.362/.542
2017	ANA	MLB	29	115	19	7	0	7	15	17	33	4	0	.245/.357/.531
2018	ANA	MLB	30	613	80	18	1	30	85	64	176	8	2	.257/.344/.463
2019	ANA	MLB	31	622	82	29	1	26	84	69	175	11	4	.248/.338/.449

Breakout: 1%   Improve: 37%   Collapse: 23%   Attrition: 8%   MLB: 99%
Comparables: Jason Bay, Mack Jones, Jason Kubel

It's easy to gloss over how much of a background staple Upton has been in the majors since his teens. He didn't set the game ablaze at 19 like Griffey or Soto, but in each season from ages 20 through 30 he's gently warmed the lineup to the core, achieving an above average OPS+. To cull a complete list of other players with that accomplishment in that age range, you'd end up with 12 Hall of Famers, Alex Rodriguez, and someone from the deadball era named Sherry Magee, which is probably made up. He's rarely an MVP candidate, sometimes an All-Star, and always consistent. The Hall of Very Good is going to have a stellar inductee in Upton when all is said and done.

YEAR	TEAM	LVL	AGE	PA	DRC+	VORP	BABIP	BRR	FRAA	WARP
2016	DET	MLB	28	626	104	16.3	.301	2.4	LF(146): -5.4, CF(6): 0.0	1.6
2017	DET	MLB	29	520	129	31.4	.351	-0.6	LF(124): 11.8	4.3
2017	ANA	MLB	29	115	131	7.6	.293	1.1	LF(27): -2.6	0.6
2018	ANA	MLB	30	613	117	33.1	.321	-1.6	LF(140): 17.0	4.4
2019	ANA	MLB	31	622	116	31.5	.315	0.0	LF 11	4.2

Justin Upton, continued

Batted Ball Distribution

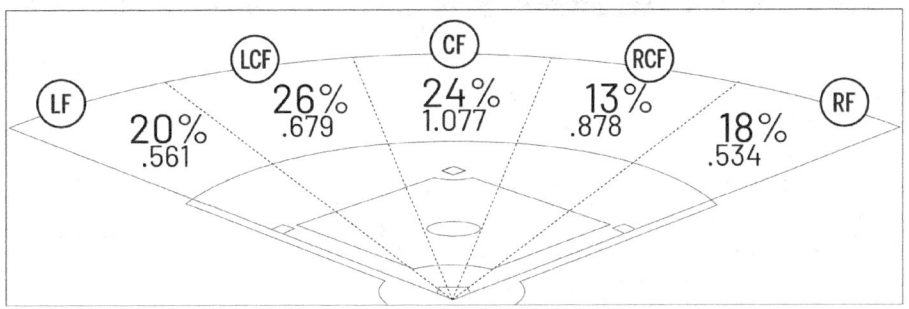

Strike Zone vs LHP   **Strike Zone vs RHP**

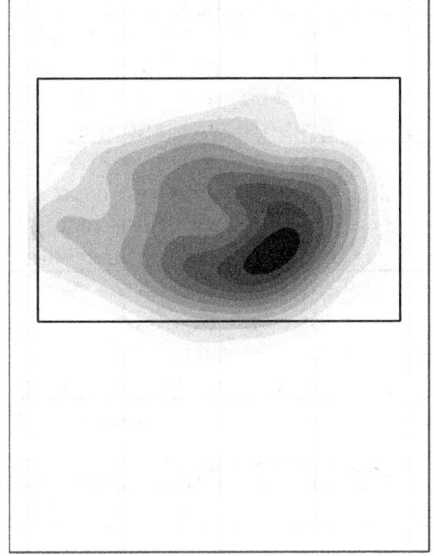

Angels Player Analysis - 45

Taylor Ward 3B

Born: 12/14/93 Age: 25 Bats: R Throws: R
Height: 6'1" Weight: 200 Origin: Round 1, 2015 Draft (#26 overall)

YEAR	TEAM	LVL	AGE	PA	R	2B	3B	HR	RBI	BB	K	SB	CS	AVG/OBP/SLG
2016	INL	A+	22	529	61	11	0	10	56	48	81	0	0	.249/.323/.337
2017	INL	A+	23	247	32	11	1	6	30	35	43	0	0	.242/.348/.391
2017	MOB	AA	23	145	14	3	0	3	19	22	17	0	0	.286/.400/.387
2018	MOB	AA	24	179	26	8	0	6	25	29	33	8	1	.345/.453/.520
2018	SLC	AAA	24	267	42	18	0	8	35	36	61	10	2	.352/.442/.537
2018	ANA	MLB	24	147	14	3	0	6	15	9	45	2	0	.178/.245/.333
2019	ANA	MLB	25	100	12	5	0	3	11	10	27	1	0	.250/.330/.409

Breakout: 8% Improve: 30% Collapse: 0% Attrition: 25% MLB: 49%
Comparables: Max Muncy, Yamaico Navarro, Conor Gillaspie

YEAR	TEAM	P. COUNT	FRM RUNS	BLK RUNS	THRW RUNS	TOT RUNS
2017	MOB	3243	-3.4	0.1	-0.1	-4.0

Three seasons after the Angels drafted him in the first round, Ward transitioned from light-hitting backstop to thumping third baseman. GM Billy Eppler and Director of Player Development Mike Gallego thought Ward would reach the majors faster if he was no longer burdened with the tools of ignorance, and boy were they right: Ward rocketed through Double-A and Triple-A, showing more power (and speed) than ever before. His transformation resulted from a series of swing tweaks to keep his bat in the zone longer and match pitch planes than through a wholesale change in approach. Always the owner of a cautious eye at the plate, Ward saw his approach exploited at the big-league level, where pitchers' elite stuff made two-strike counts more dangerous than ever. While the switch to the hot corner saw him improve at the plate, the his work at third could still use some editing. He doesn't lack for athleticism, but is still raw, resulting in 17 errors between the three levels he saw last year. Further refinement in the field to complement his progress at the plate could see Ward solidify himself as an everyday player.

YEAR	TEAM	LVL	AGE	PA	DRC+	VORP	BABIP	BRR	FRAA	WARP
2016	INL	A+	22	529	97	9.4	.279	1.4	C(90): 4.2	1.2
2017	INL	A+	23	247	110	11.2	.275	1.3	C(42): -0.8	0.6
2017	MOB	AA	23	145	160	11.5	.307	0.3	C(21): -3.9	0.8
2018	MOB	AA	24	179	187	19.7	.409	-1.6	3B(33): -2.8	1.4
2018	SLC	AAA	24	267	150	16.9	.450	-4.4	3B(53): -10.4	0.6
2018	ANA	MLB	24	147	77	-4.2	.214	-2.4	3B(40): -2.3	-0.4
2019	ANA	MLB	25	100	101	2.6	.319	0.0	3B -3	0.0

Taylor Ward, continued

Batted Ball Distribution

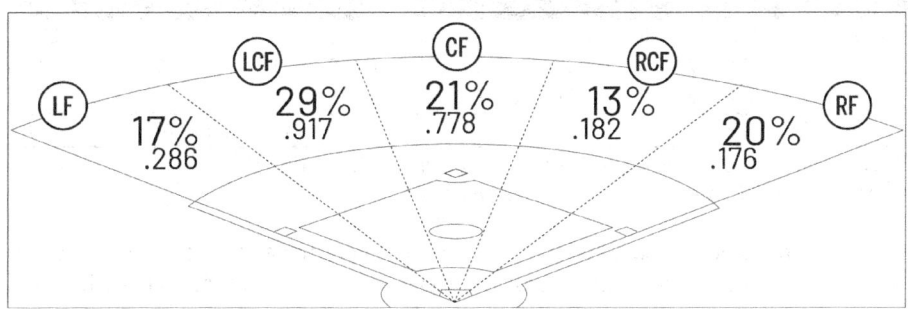

Strike Zone vs LHP   Strike Zone vs RHP

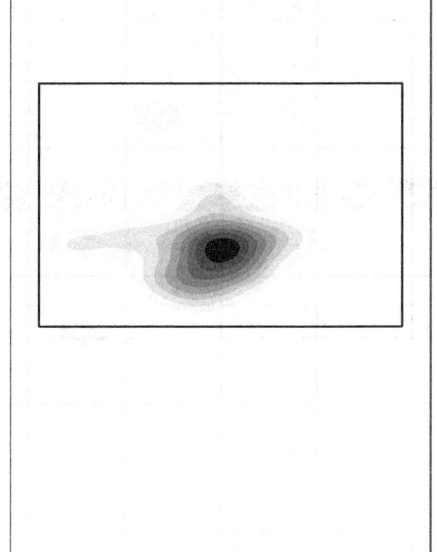

Angels Player Analysis - 47

Cody Allen RHP

Born: 11/20/88   Age: 30   Bats: R   Throws: R
Height: 6'1"   Weight: 210   Origin: Round 23, 2011 Draft (#698 overall)

YEAR	TEAM	LVL	AGE	W	L	SV	G	GS	IP	H	HR	BB/9	K/9	K	GB%	BABIP
2016	CLE	MLB	27	3	5	32	67	0	68	41	8	3.6	11.5	87	48%	.232
2017	CLE	MLB	28	3	7	30	69	0	67[1]	57	9	2.8	12.3	92	34%	.304
2018	CLE	MLB	29	4	6	27	70	0	67	58	11	4.4	10.7	80	31%	.292
2019	ANA	MLB	30	3	3	32	59	0	62	54	9	4.0	10.1	70	38%	.284

Breakout: 19%   Improve: 36%   Collapse: 39%   Attrition: 10%   MLB: 95%
Comparables: Kyle Farnsworth, Armando Benitez, Brad Lidge

Conventional wisdom says relievers are volatile year to year, and players in their primes tend to give their best performances in contract years. Allen is a bit of a contrarian, it seems. Since Barack Obama's first term, Allen had never had a season with an ERA over 3.00, and had only one year with a DRA over 3.00, pairing mid-90s heat with a vicious curveball to rack up nearly 100 strikeouts a year out of the bullpen. Unfortunately, Allen picked his contract year to let his run-prevention numbers spike. His velocity has now dropped five consecutive seasons, but there should still be enough for him to be effective. Although his peripherals also took a step backward last year, it wasn't as ugly as his ERA suggests. It's probably safe to guess his decline phase has arrived, but it may be a gentle slide from a very great height.

YEAR	TEAM	LVL	AGE	WHIP	ERA	DRA	WARP	MPH	FB%	WHF	CSP
2016	CLE	MLB	27	1.00	2.51	2.90	1.6	96.5	63.3	14.4	45.9
2017	CLE	MLB	28	1.16	2.94	2.64	1.9	95.5	55.5	15.5	41.8
2018	CLE	MLB	29	1.36	4.70	3.61	1.0	94.9	60.3	13.9	43.1
2019	ANA	MLB	30	1.29	4.37	4.44	0.5	94.7	59.2	14.5	43.2

Cody Allen, continued

Pitch Shape vs LHH

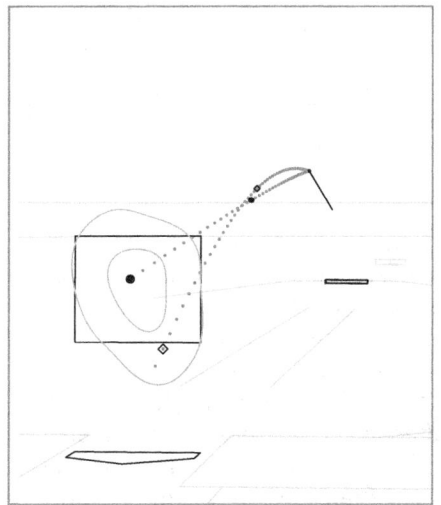

Pitch Shape vs RHH

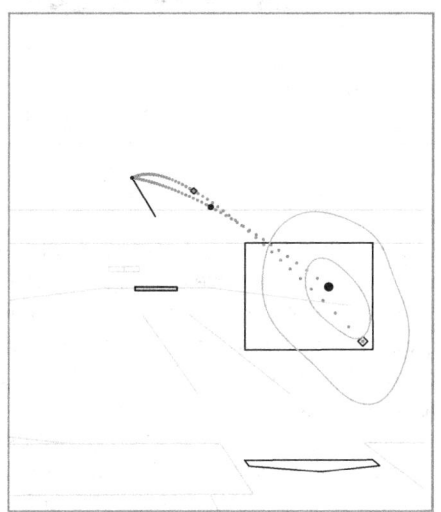

Type	Frequency	Velocity	H Movement	V Movement
● Fastball	60.3%	94 [105]	-8.4 [92]	-11.4 [114]
☐ Sinker				
+ Cutter				
▲ Changeup				
✕ Splitter				
▽ Slider				
◇ Curveball	39.7%	83.8 [120]	8.6 [103]	-41.5 [115]
✦ Slow Curveball				
✶ Knuckleball				
▼ Screwball				

Angels Player Analysis - 49

Justin Anderson RHP

Born: 09/28/92 Age: 26 Bats: L Throws: R
Height: 6'3" Weight: 220 Origin: Round 14, 2014 Draft (#419 overall)

YEAR	TEAM	LVL	AGE	W	L	SV	G	GS	IP	H	HR	BB/9	K/9	K	GB%	BABIP
2016	INL	A+	23	8	12	0	28	27	145^1	193	15	3.0	6.6	107	44%	.368
2017	MOB	AA	24	3	2	1	42	0	58^2	56	7	4.4	5.5	36	49%	.266
2018	ANA	MLB	25	3	3	4	57	0	55^1	42	3	6.5	10.9	67	54%	.310
2019	ANA	MLB	26	3	3	3	59	0	62	54	6	4.8	9.8	69	46%	.295

Breakout: 22% Improve: 32% Collapse: 9% Attrition: 25% MLB: 46%
Comparables: Matt Marksberry, J.D. Durbin, Frank Garces

Two years ago, Anderson was a Double-A power righty with awful command who couldn't generate outs, so you can blame him for not being in our book. While we were copyediting, he was delivery-editing. His seven scoreless appearances in spring training turned heads (despite no official invite) and he followed it up with blanks in Double-A and Triple-A. He snuck into the Angels' bullpen by late April, much in part to those ahead of him visiting the infirmary. His fastball peaked at 99 (though not as often late in the season) and his slider transformed into a more deceptive out pitch. When all was said and done he had the best K/9 of any Angel except for that Ohtani guy. They came at a cost, however, as his BB/9 nearly doubled the league average. He limits extra-base hits and doesn't show much of a platoon preference, so he'll stick around long enough for attentive fans to remember the name.

YEAR	TEAM	LVL	AGE	WHIP	ERA	DRA	WARP	MPH	FB%	WHF	CSP
2016	INL	A+	23	1.66	5.70	6.73	-2.1				
2017	MOB	AA	24	1.45	5.06	5.87	-0.8				
2018	ANA	MLB	25	1.48	4.07	4.52	0.3	99.2	44.7	14.4	42.2
2019	ANA	MLB	26	1.40	4.06	4.18	0.7	98.8	45.5	14.6	42.9

Justin Anderson, continued

Pitch Shape vs LHH

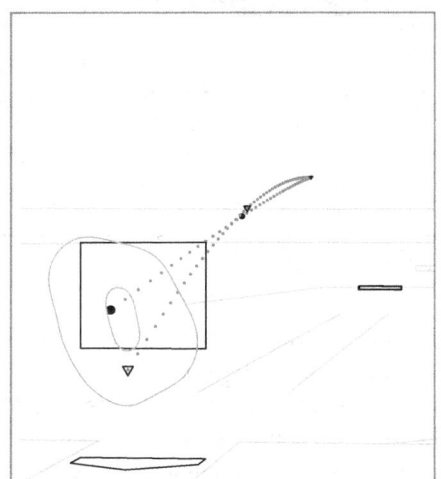

Pitch Shape vs RHH

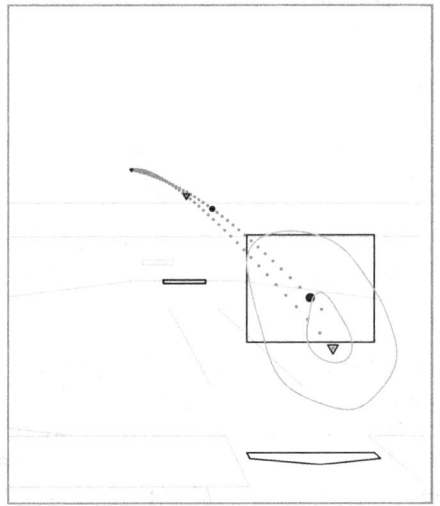

Type	Frequency	Velocity	H Movement	V Movement
● Fastball	44.6%	97.8 [117]	-8.3 [92]	-12.2 [111]
☐ Sinker	0.1%	96.8 [122]	-10.7 [116]	-15.8 [115]
+ Cutter				
▲ Changeup	0.3%	86.9 [106]	-10.5 [104]	-22.3 [115]
✕ Splitter				
▽ Slider	54.7%	86.1 [107]	8.3 [115]	-32.7 [101]
◇ Curveball	0.4%	80.5 [108]	12.1 [118]	-43.4 [110]
⊕ Slow Curveball				
✱ Knuckleball				
▼ Screwball				

Jaime Barria   RHP

Born: 07/18/96 Age: 22 Bats: R Throws: R
Height: 6'1" Weight: 210 Origin: International Free Agent, 2013

YEAR	TEAM	LVL	AGE	W	L	SV	G	GS	IP	H	HR	BB/9	K/9	K	GB%	BABIP
2016	BUR	A	19	8	6	0	25	25	117	133	6	1.6	6.0	78	44%	.323
2017	INL	A+	20	4	3	0	11	11	65^1	48	6	1.8	7.9	57	35%	.236
2017	MOB	AA	20	1	6	0	12	12	61^2	62	8	2.2	6.9	47	29%	.284
2017	SLC	AAA	20	2	0	0	3	3	14^2	11	0	1.8	8.0	13	29%	.262
2018	SLC	AAA	21	0	0	0	5	5	18	20	2	2.5	9.5	19	28%	.353
2018	ANA	MLB	21	10	9	0	26	26	129^1	117	17	3.3	6.8	98	37%	.272
2019	ANA	MLB	22	7	7	0	21	21	111^1	112	20	3.0	7.5	93	36%	.286

Breakout: 17%   Improve: 26%   Collapse: 12%   Attrition: 19%   MLB: 50%
Comparables: Mat Latos, Drew Hutchison, Jacob Turner

Be thankful you're not getting a riff on Santana's "Maria, Maria" here. This west coast story's stage was set last year when Barria blew through three levels of the minor leagues, priming him to make his major-league debut at the tender age of 21. Not bad for a $60,000 investment by the Angels. He pitched well despite riding the bus from Salt Lake City to Anaheim throughout the first half of the season, suppressing offense despite the lack of a bat-missing pitch. Barria wasn't the type of prospect to generate a ton of buzz, because he was more about location and weak contact than elite stuff. But with a bevy of average-or-better offerings and advanced control he more than held his own in his inaugural season as a major leaguer. He relied heavily on his slider to mask his non-elite heater, but he has the flexibility to mix in his change more often if the league adapts. He might not generate a ton of headlines, but Barria should find himself taking regular rotation turns for the foreseeable future.

YEAR	TEAM	LVL	AGE	WHIP	ERA	DRA	WARP	MPH	FB%	WHF	CSP
2016	BUR	A	19	1.32	3.85	3.72	1.8				
2017	INL	A+	20	0.93	2.48	4.31	0.7				
2017	MOB	AA	20	1.25	3.21	3.25	1.4				
2017	SLC	AAA	20	0.95	2.45	3.61	0.3				
2018	SLC	AAA	21	1.39	3.50	4.64	0.2				
2018	ANA	MLB	21	1.27	3.41	5.67	-0.5	92.8	49.6	11.2	45
2019	ANA	MLB	22	1.32	5.04	5.22	0.3	92.8	51.7	11.7	46.9

Jaime Barria, continued

Pitch Shape vs LHH

Pitch Shape vs RHH

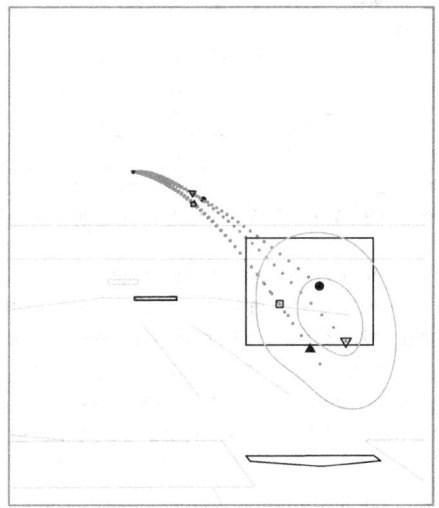

Type	Frequency	Velocity	H Movement	V Movement
● Fastball	38.3%	91.7 [97]	-5.9 [104]	-13.8 [106]
☐ Sinker	11.3%	91.2 [94]	-10.4 [118]	-16.1 [114]
+ Cutter				
▲ Changeup	14.0%	83 [91]	-9.1 [112]	-26.4 [103]
✕ Splitter				
▽ Slider	36.5%	82.2 [90]	2.4 [89]	-31.8 [104]
◇ Curveball				
⊕ Slow Curveball				
✱ Knuckleball				
▼ Screwball				

Angels Player Analysis - 53

Cam Bedrosian RHP

Born: 10/02/91 Age: 27 Bats: R Throws: R
Height: 6'0" Weight: 230 Origin: Round 1, 2010 Draft (#29 overall)

YEAR	TEAM	LVL	AGE	W	L	SV	G	GS	IP	H	HR	BB/9	K/9	K	GB%	BABIP
2016	SLC	AAA	24	1	0	1	5	0	8^1	7	1	4.3	15.1	14	53%	.333
2016	ANA	MLB	24	2	0	1	45	0	40^1	30	1	3.1	11.4	51	52%	.309
2017	ANA	MLB	25	6	5	6	48	0	44^2	41	5	3.4	10.7	53	45%	.313
2018	ANA	MLB	26	5	4	1	71	0	64	63	7	3.7	8.0	57	50%	.315
2019	ANA	MLB	27	3	3	0	54	0	57	54	7	3.9	8.8	56	47%	.298

Breakout: 35% Improve: 54% Collapse: 20% Attrition: 17% MLB: 93%
Comparables: Kyle McClellan, Brian Bruney, Manny Delcarmen

Steve's kid had by far his biggest workload, but perhaps not coincidentally, also his slowest fastball. It could still beat Jered Weaver's in a footrace with its seams tied behind its back, but Bedrosian averaged fewer than a punchout per frame for the first time in his career. That's a fireballer's worst nightmare this side of a changeup marrying their mother. Even if the heater stays a modest 93 he's a durable reliever, but his days as emergency-closer-in-waiting might be behind him.

YEAR	TEAM	LVL	AGE	WHIP	ERA	DRA	WARP	MPH	FB%	WHF	CSP
2016	SLC	AAA	24	1.32	3.24	1.99	0.3				
2016	ANA	MLB	24	1.09	1.12	3.14	0.8	97.6	67.7	11.7	46.7
2017	ANA	MLB	25	1.30	4.43	2.97	1.1	95.4	57.7	13.5	46.5
2018	ANA	MLB	26	1.39	3.80	4.21	0.5	95.1	55.5	8.6	47.9
2019	ANA	MLB	27	1.38	4.31	4.39	0.5	95.2	59.2	10.8	47.7

Cam Bedrosian, continued

Pitch Shape vs LHH

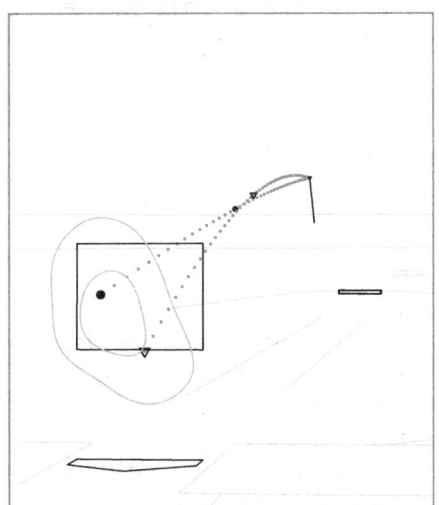

Pitch Shape vs RHH

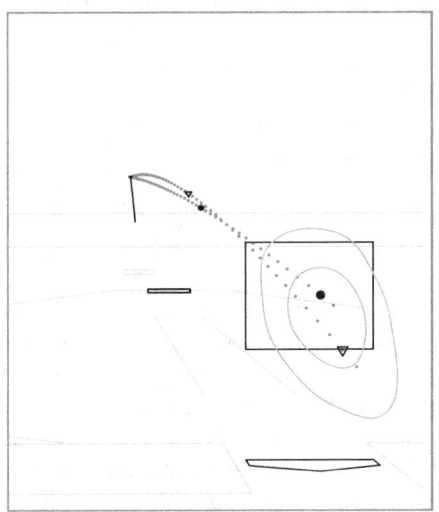

Type	Frequency	Velocity	H Movement	V Movement
● Fastball	55.4%	93.6 [104]	-1.4 [124]	-13.1 [108]
□ Sinker	0.1%	92.2 [99]	-10.6 [116]	-19.6 [102]
+ Cutter				
▲ Changeup				
✕ Splitter				
▽ Slider	44.6%	83.5 [96]	7.4 [111]	-41.3 [76]
◇ Curveball				
✥ Slow Curveball				
✱ Knuckleball				
▼ Screwball				

Ty Buttrey   RHP

Born: 03/31/93   Age: 26   Bats: L   Throws: R
Height: 6'6"   Weight: 230   Origin: Round 4, 2012 Draft (#151 overall)

YEAR	TEAM	LVL	AGE	W	L	SV	G	GS	IP	H	HR	BB/9	K/9	K	GB%	BABIP
2016	PME	AA	23	1	9	0	33	9	79	80	6	5.2	5.9	52	52%	.292
2017	PAW	AAA	24	1	1	0	10	0	17^2	21	2	5.1	9.2	18	53%	.358
2017	PME	AA	24	1	4	4	30	0	46	39	1	4.5	11.0	56	50%	.339
2018	PAW	AAA	25	1	1	1	32	0	44	36	4	2.9	13.1	64	45%	.320
2018	ANA	MLB	25	0	1	4	16	0	16^1	15	0	2.8	11.0	20	58%	.333
2019	ANA	MLB	26	3	3	6	54	0	57	47	5	4.4	10.2	65	47%	.292

Breakout: 15%   Improve: 29%   Collapse: 7%   Attrition: 20%   MLB: 45%
Comparables: Tom Mastny, Davis Romero, Patrick Light

If you flip through previous editions of the Annual to look at Boston's 2012 overslot signing, you'll note a common theme: Buttrey issues too many free passes. Just last year we said he'd be stuck in Triple-A until he could cut down on the walks, so we'll just go ahead and assume he read the book. He finally broke through in 2018, reaching the majors to buttress the Angels' crumbling bullpen. His insistent fastball cut through opposing lineups like a hot knife through one of those midwestern gelatin salads, and he did a great job of keeping the ball on the ground in a small sample. He missed bats with his changeup (14 percent whiff rate) and slider (24 percent), and if he can maintain his ground-ball and strikeout rates, he can expect to be a mainstay in the bullpen.

YEAR	TEAM	LVL	AGE	WHIP	ERA	DRA	WARP	MPH	FB%	WHF	CSP
2016	PME	AA	23	1.59	4.44	4.41	0.5				
2017	PAW	AAA	24	1.75	7.64	3.41	0.4				
2017	PME	AA	24	1.35	3.72	3.56	0.7				
2018	PAW	AAA	25	1.14	2.25	2.65	1.2				
2018	ANA	MLB	25	1.22	3.31	2.90	0.4	98.2	58	14	47.3
2019	ANA	MLB	26	1.32	3.71	3.90	0.8	97.8	59	14.3	48.1

Ty Buttrey, continued

Pitch Shape vs LHH

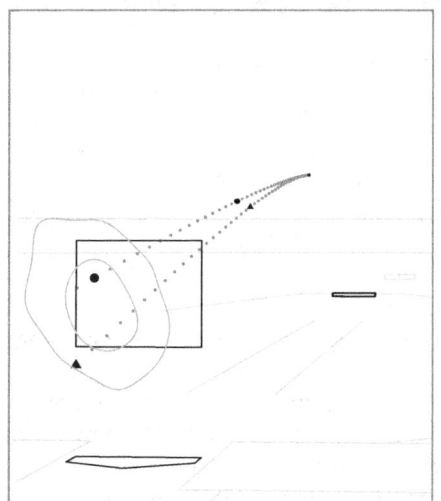

Pitch Shape vs RHH

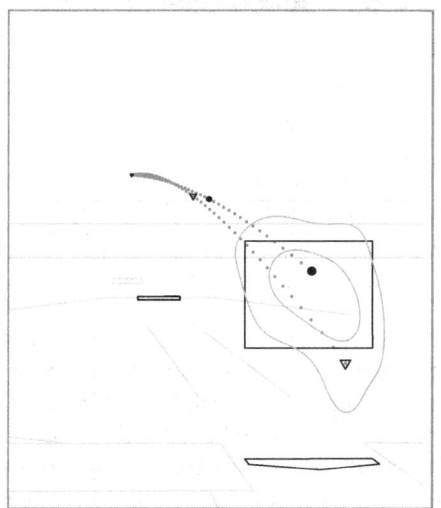

Type	Frequency	Velocity	H Movement	V Movement
● Fastball	58.0%	96.4 [113]	-10.8 [81]	-13.8 [106]
□ Sinker				
+ Cutter				
▲ Changeup	16.7%	86.5 [105]	-15.3 [78]	-29.9 [92]
× Splitter				
▽ Slider	25.3%	82.4 [91]	0.2 [80]	-37.3 [87]
◇ Curveball				
⊕ Slow Curveball				
✱ Knuckleball				
▼ Screwball				

Trevor Cahill RHP

Born: 03/01/88 Age: 31 Bats: R Throws: R
Height: 6'4" Weight: 240 Origin: Round 2, 2006 Draft (#66 overall)

YEAR	TEAM	LVL	AGE	W	L	SV	G	GS	IP	H	HR	BB/9	K/9	K	GB%	BABIP
2016	IOW	AAA	28	0	3	0	6	6	19²	25	3	5.5	11.4	25	53%	.407
2016	CHN	MLB	28	4	4	0	50	1	65²	49	7	4.8	9.0	66	57%	.246
2017	SDN	MLB	29	4	3	0	11	11	61	58	6	3.5	10.6	72	58%	.329
2017	KCA	MLB	29	0	0	0	10	3	23	33	10	8.2	5.9	15	54%	.319
2018	NAS	AAA	30	0	1	0	3	3	13²	7	0	5.3	11.2	17	81%	.226
2018	OAK	MLB	30	7	4	0	21	20	110	90	8	3.4	8.2	100	54%	.278
2019	ANA	MLB	31	7	7	0	21	21	111¹	105	14	4.1	8.4	104	53%	.293

Breakout: 24% Improve: 49% Collapse: 19% Attrition: 15% MLB: 87%
Comparables: Tom Koehler, Sam LeCure, David Phelps

Cahill was the other half of the prodigal duo brought back to Oakland last year, along with Brett Anderson. In his years in the wilderness, the only constant was inconsistency, which led to him being available in mid-March for $1.5 million after Jharel Cotton hurt his elbow. Cahill had seen the usual velocity bump upon his move to the bullpen, adding about two mph to his sinker; the most intriguing part of his 2018 performance was that he kept that bump in Oakland's rotation. This helped him place among the top quartile of starting pitchers in the Statcast "barrel" measures (which attempt to capture how often batters make solid contact), near pitchers like Patrick Corbin and Max Scherzer. Cahill would need to add whiffs or cut walks (or both) to reach that type of elite status overall, and that's not going to happen, but avoiding hard contact could keep him in the league for a few more years, especially if he keeps pitching in front of top-notch defensive infields.

YEAR	TEAM	LVL	AGE	WHIP	ERA	DRA	WARP	MPH	FB%	WHF	CSP
2016	IOW	AAA	28	1.88	4.58	2.32	0.7				
2016	CHN	MLB	28	1.28	2.74	4.14	0.7	95.1	54.5	11.6	40.4
2017	SDN	MLB	29	1.34	3.69	3.51	1.4	93.1	45.7	13.4	42.4
2017	KCA	MLB	29	2.35	8.22	6.61	-0.3	93.3	50	7.3	41.7
2018	NAS	AAA	30	1.10	2.63	1.65	0.6				
2018	OAK	MLB	30	1.19	3.76	3.48	2.3	93.8	41.1	12.1	44.5
2019	ANA	MLB	31	1.39	4.52	4.65	1.0	93.0	45.3	11.7	42.4

Trevor Cahill, continued

Pitch Shape vs LHH

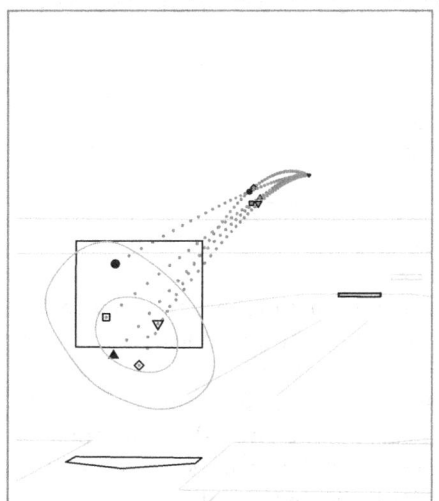

Pitch Shape vs RHH

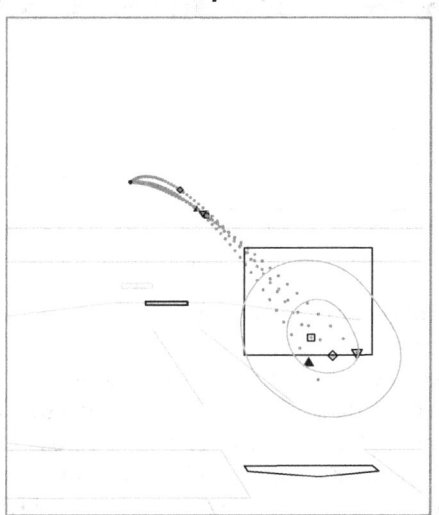

Type	Frequency	Velocity	H Movement	V Movement
● Fastball	3.1%	93.2 [102]	-8.2 [93]	-15.2 [102]
□ Sinker	38.0%	92.4 [100]	-14.5 [84]	-22.6 [93]
+ Cutter				
▲ Changeup	24.3%	84.6 [97]	-11.1 [101]	-34.8 [78]
× Splitter				
▽ Slider	18.9%	88.5 [118]	-0.3 [78]	-25.3 [123]
◇ Curveball	15.7%	80.9 [109]	8.4 [102]	-47.3 [102]
⊕ Slow Curveball				
✶ Knuckleball				
▼ Screwball				

Angels Player Analysis - 59

Taylor Cole RHP

Born: 08/20/89 Age: 29 Bats: R Throws: R
Height: 6'1" Weight: 200 Origin: Round 29, 2011 Draft (#889 overall)

YEAR	TEAM	LVL	AGE	W	L	SV	G	GS	IP	H	HR	BB/9	K/9	K	GB%	BABIP
2016	DUN	A+	26	1	0	0	3	3	15^1	20	0	1.8	4.7	8	59%	.370
2016	NHP	AA	26	3	4	0	12	11	61^2	70	6	2.5	7.9	54	51%	.352
2017	TOR	MLB	27	0	0	0	1	0	1	6	0	9.0	9.0	1	57%	.857
2018	SLC	AAA	28	3	0	6	34	0	55^1	55	6	4.4	10.6	65	48%	.343
2018	ANA	MLB	28	4	2	0	18	2	36	20	3	3.0	9.8	39	52%	.218
2019	ANA	MLB	29	3	3	0	37	5	59^1	53	7	3.9	9.4	62	47%	.296

Breakout: 8% Improve: 11% Collapse: 13% Attrition: 14% MLB: 34%
Comparables: Ramon A. Ramirez, Brian Slocum, Alex Wimmers

Cole spent seven nondescript seasons in the Blue Jays organization before being given the ol' Toronto Toodle-loo. Last year he shuttled between Anaheim and Salt Lake, posting some curiously minuscule numbers, in the good way, for a team desperate for a warm body that knew how to hurl hard spheres. It's an average three-pitch repertoire across the board, though he'll throw any of the three in any count, and the advanced mixology shook out to a solid count of whiffs and grounders alike. The low ERA might have been a bit fortuitous, given the BABIP, though if everything works out he could start some late-summer games as the infirmary fills up. For now, he's a multi-inning relief option.

YEAR	TEAM	LVL	AGE	WHIP	ERA	DRA	WARP	MPH	FB%	WHF	CSP
2016	DUN	A+	26	1.50	4.70	4.33	0.2				
2016	NHP	AA	26	1.41	3.79	3.95	0.8				
2017	TOR	MLB	27	7.00	36.00	11.11	-0.1	95.3	58.5	9.8	43.2
2018	SLC	AAA	28	1.48	5.37	3.88	0.8				
2018	ANA	MLB	28	0.89	2.75	4.24	0.3	95.1	39.1	15.9	41.8
2019	ANA	MLB	29	1.33	4.16	4.27	0.7	94.4	40.1	15.6	42.4

Taylor Cole, continued

Pitch Shape vs LHH
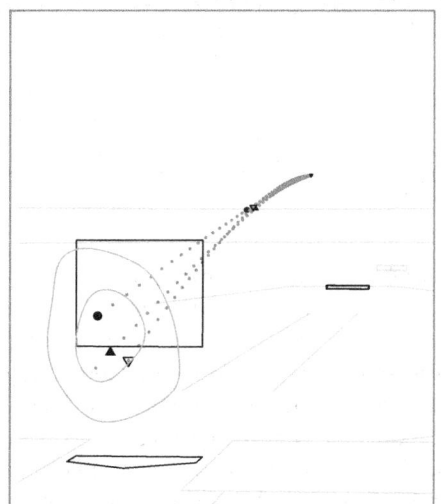

Pitch Shape vs RHH
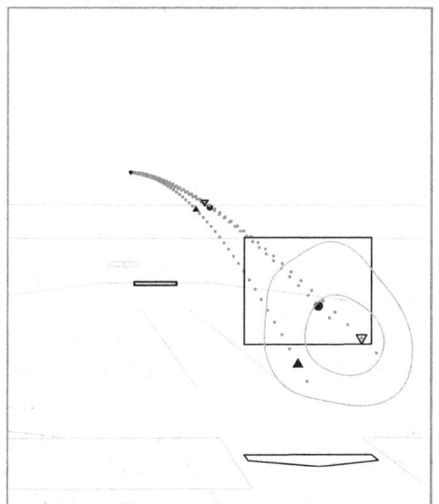

Type	Frequency	Velocity	H Movement	V Movement
● Fastball	39.1%	93.3 [103]	-10.4 [83]	-14.8 [103]
☐ Sinker				
+ Cutter	2.6%	91.4 [116]	-1.1 [82]	-17.1 [127]
▲ Changeup	23.5%	87.2 [107]	-11.6 [98]	-28.3 [97]
✕ Splitter				
▽ Slider	34.9%	86.9 [111]	1.7 [87]	-27.3 [117]
◇ Curveball				
✦ Slow Curveball				
✳ Knuckleball				
▼ Screwball				

Luis Garcia   RHP

Born: 01/30/87   Age: 32   Bats: R   Throws: R
Height: 6'3"   Weight: 230   Origin: International Free Agent, 2017

YEAR	TEAM	LVL	AGE	W	L	SV	G	GS	IP	H	HR	BB/9	K/9	K	GB%	BABIP
2016	LEH	AAA	29	6	3	13	48	0	54²	38	3	4.0	8.7	53	63%	.261
2016	PHI	MLB	29	1	1	0	17	0	15¹	21	2	4.7	8.2	14	55%	.373
2017	PHI	MLB	30	2	5	2	66	0	71¹	61	3	3.3	7.6	60	57%	.282
2018	PHI	MLB	31	3	1	1	59	0	46	49	4	3.5	10.0	51	50%	.354
2019	ANA	MLB	32	3	3	0	54	0	57	52	7	4.3	9.0	57	51%	.294

Breakout: 23%   Improve: 41%   Collapse: 24%   Attrition: 20%   MLB: 78%
Comparables: Saul Rivera, Ryan Mattheus, Joe Beimel

Luis Garcia—or, I should say, the *idea* of Luis Garcia—doesn't make any sense. Bakc in 2014, Garcia emerged from the minors with a high-90s heater and buckling splitter, the same two-pitch combo propelling Hector Neris to success. That he'd added five ticks on his fastball midseason was striking, and seemingly positioned him well to hold down a bullpen spot in 2015. And while the velocity has held in the years since, Garcia's performance has been anything but predictable. Garcia managed to trim his walk rate below nine percent while bumping his strikeouts up to 25 percent in 2018—career-best numbers in both cases—but also got hit harder than ever in exchange. The end result is a negative RE24 for the fifth time in six seasons. It was an unlucky turn given the under-the-hood indicators. He under-performed his DRA by a larger margin than any other pitcher in baseball who matched his innings, and the Angels made a big bet that his actual 2019 will look more like his theoretical 2018 when they shipped their only reliable lefty reliever to Philly to get him.

YEAR	TEAM	LVL	AGE	WHIP	ERA	DRA	WARP	MPH	FB%	WHF	CSP
2016	LEH	AAA	29	1.13	2.14	3.40	1.0				
2016	PHI	MLB	29	1.89	6.46	4.65	0.1	99.0	57.3	11.8	44.1
2017	PHI	MLB	30	1.22	2.65	3.26	1.5	98.7	63.3	12.8	49
2018	PHI	MLB	31	1.46	6.07	3.25	0.9	99.2	48.4	15.5	44.8
2019	ANA	MLB	32	1.39	4.45	4.50	0.4	97.9	55.6	13.7	45.6

Luis Garcia, continued

Pitch Shape vs LHH

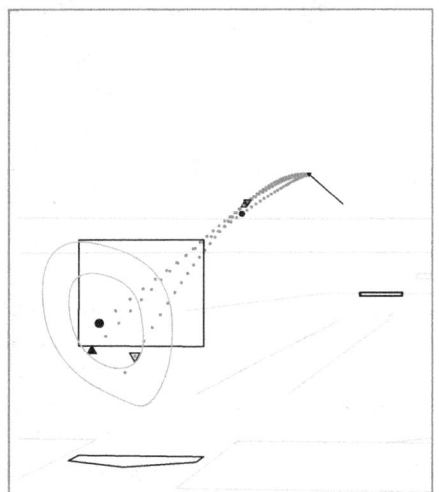

Pitch Shape vs RHH

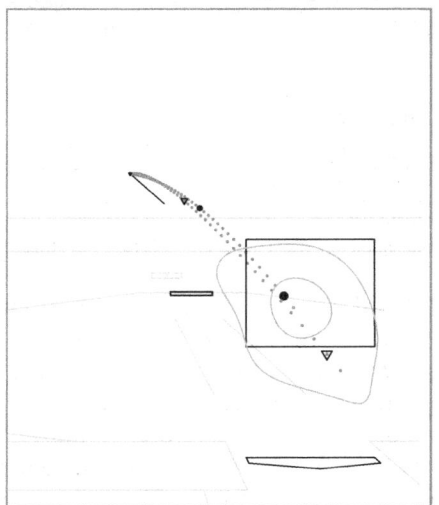

Type	Frequency	Velocity	H Movement	V Movement
● Fastball	48.4%	97.8 [117]	-10.7 [81]	-16.3 [98]
□ Sinker				
+ Cutter				
▲ Changeup	11.9%	87.5 [109]	-5.8 [129]	-29.2 [94]
× Splitter				
▽ Slider	39.7%	85.4 [104]	7.9 [113]	-33.2 [99]
◇ Curveball				
✦ Slow Curveball				
✷ Knuckleball				
▼ Screwball				

Los Angeles Angels 2019

Matt Harvey RHP

Born: 03/27/89 Age: 30 Bats: R Throws: R
Height: 6'4" Weight: 215 Origin: Round 1, 2010 Draft (#7 overall)

YEAR	TEAM	LVL	AGE	W	L	SV	G	GS	IP	H	HR	BB/9	K/9	K	GB%	BABIP
2016	NYN	MLB	27	4	10	0	17	17	92^2	111	8	2.4	7.4	76	44%	.353
2017	BIN	AA	28	0	0	0	2	2	7^2	9	1	2.3	5.9	5	33%	.308
2017	NYN	MLB	28	5	7	0	19	18	92^2	110	21	4.6	6.5	67	46%	.307
2018	NYN	MLB	29	0	2	0	8	4	27	33	6	3.0	6.7	20	43%	.310
2018	CIN	MLB	29	7	7	0	24	24	128	132	21	2.0	7.8	111	46%	.296
2019	ANA	MLB	30	6	6	0	19	19	100^2	104	16	3.0	7.4	83	44%	.295

Breakout: 23%   Improve: 53%   Collapse: 7%   Attrition: 9%   MLB: 84%
Comparables: Chris Capuano, Paul Derringer, Ricky Nolasco

It's hard to watch Harvey today without reflecting on all that's come before: the flight and the fall, the scowls and scars and bitterness and whispers and general cussedness that's surrounded the man. Yet we shouldn't lose track of the odds that he has beaten to return from elbow ligament and thoracic outlet surgery as a usable major league starter. When he's right, Harvey can still dial his fastball into the mid-90s and his slider still darts and dives. When he's not right, and like most back-end starters that happens a lot, lefty power bats take him to the woodshed. He's a solid number four with some upside remaining, and there's a non-zero chance that putting another winter between Harvey and the operating room will tease out a little more of the old magic. The Angels, believing in magic, signed him for a year at $11 million.

YEAR	TEAM	LVL	AGE	WHIP	ERA	DRA	WARP	MPH	FB%	WHF	CSP
2016	NYN	MLB	27	1.47	4.86	3.57	1.9	97.4	60	10.9	48.8
2017	BIN	AA	28	1.43	5.87	6.43	-0.1				
2017	NYN	MLB	28	1.69	6.70	6.63	-1.1	95.9	59.3	8.6	47
2018	NYN	MLB	29	1.56	7.00	4.18	0.3	94.4	61.2	8.2	49.7
2018	CIN	MLB	29	1.25	4.50	4.79	0.7	96.2	58.7	10.4	53
2019	ANA	MLB	30	1.37	4.82	4.98	0.5	95.4	59.2	9.8	49.5

Matt Harvey, continued

Pitch Shape vs LHH

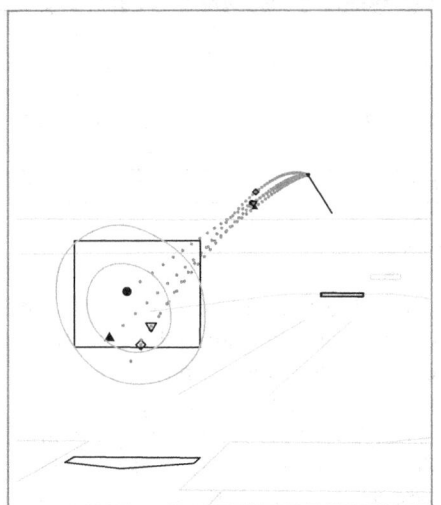

Pitch Shape vs RHH

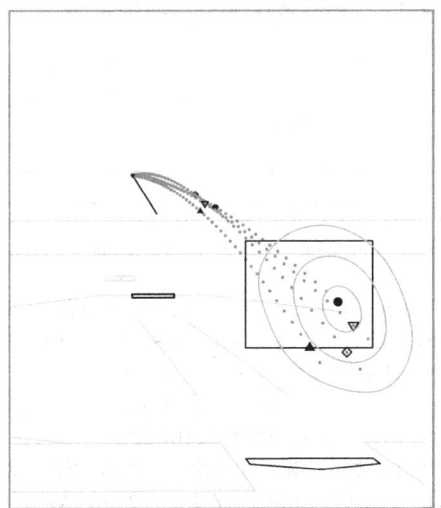

Type	Frequency	Velocity	H Movement	V Movement
● Fastball	58.7%	94.7 [107]	-9.9 [85]	-15.1 [102]
☐ Sinker	0.4%	93.1 [103]	-12.9 [97]	-20.3 [100]
+ Cutter				
▲ Changeup	11.5%	87.8 [110]	-12.2 [95]	-22.7 [114]
✕ Splitter				
▽ Slider	23.9%	89.1 [121]	2 [87]	-25 [124]
◇ Curveball	5.5%	83.4 [118]	1.8 [75]	-39.5 [119]
⊕ Slow Curveball				
✳ Knuckleball				
▼ Screwball				

Andrew Heaney LHP

Born: 06/05/91   Age: 28   Bats: L   Throws: L
Height: 6'2"   Weight: 185   Origin: Round 1, 2012 Draft (#9 overall)

YEAR	TEAM	LVL	AGE	W	L	SV	G	GS	IP	H	HR	BB/9	K/9	K	GB%	BABIP
2016	ANA	MLB	25	0	1	0	1	1	6	7	2	0.0	10.5	7	44%	.312
2017	ANG	RK	26	0	1	0	3	3	10^1	11	0	0.9	13.1	15	42%	.423
2017	SLC	AAA	26	1	1	0	3	3	17^1	17	2	2.1	7.3	14	39%	.306
2017	ANA	MLB	26	1	2	0	5	5	21^2	27	12	3.7	11.2	27	34%	.283
2018	ANA	MLB	27	9	10	0	30	30	180	171	27	2.2	9.0	180	44%	.294
2019	ANA	MLB	28	7	7	0	21	21	119^2	115	21	3.4	9.1	121	43%	.291

Breakout: 27%   Improve: 58%   Collapse: 8%   Attrition: 15%   MLB: 90%
Comparables: Zach McAllister, John Maine, Chase Anderson

Heaney is a wiry left-hander who finally assembled a complete season without any screws flying out the side in comical Hanna-Barbera fashion. He was way up the charts in terms of limiting hard contact on average and even tossed a one-hitter for good measure. For someone who doesn't burn the radar guns (he sits mostly at 92), many of those strikeouts are attributed to his curveball, arguably the best breaking pitch from the sinister side except for perhaps Blake Snell's curve. His bugaboo, as is the case with many soft-tossers, is the longball: over half his runs allowed were via the dinger. It's hard to find patterns in a record as spotty as Heaney's, and you'd like to believe that he can improve on his mistakes, but baseball has swallowed whole the careers of those much better than him.

YEAR	TEAM	LVL	AGE	WHIP	ERA	DRA	WARP	MPH	FB%	WHF	CSP
2016	ANA	MLB	25	1.17	6.00	5.15	0.0	94.3	58.6	14.9	46
2017	ANG	RK	26	1.16	1.74	1.56	0.5				
2017	SLC	AAA	26	1.21	3.12	4.38	0.3				
2017	ANA	MLB	26	1.66	7.06	5.71	0.0	94.2	61.6	14.6	44.5
2018	ANA	MLB	27	1.20	4.15	3.63	3.5	94.2	58.1	12.7	50.8
2019	ANA	MLB	28	1.32	4.77	4.93	0.7	93.6	58.8	13.1	47.8

Andrew Heaney, continued

Pitch Shape vs LHH

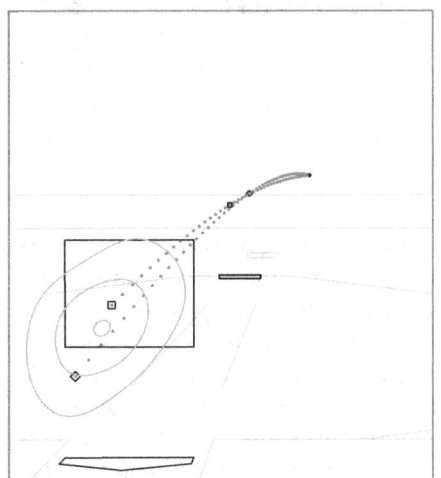

Pitch Shape vs RHH

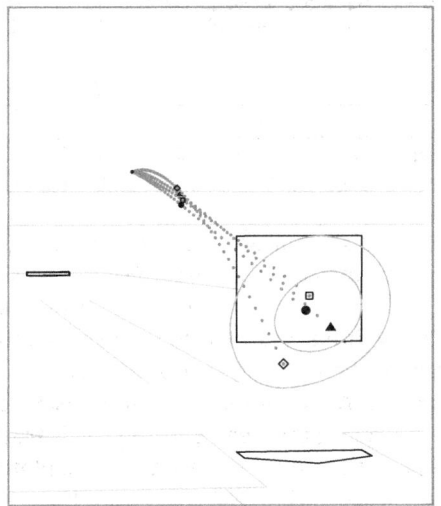

Type	Frequency	Velocity	H Movement	V Movement
● Fastball	2.0%	92.5 [100]	12.7 [72]	-16.6 [97]
□ Sinker	56.2%	92.4 [100]	12.5 [101]	-16.5 [113]
+ Cutter				
▲ Changeup	16.6%	83.8 [94]	14.8 [81]	-28.8 [96]
× Splitter				
▽ Slider				
◇ Curveball	25.2%	79 [102]	-3.7 [82]	-42.5 [113]
✣ Slow Curveball				
✱ Knuckleball				
▼ Screwball				

Angels Player Analysis - 67

Daniel Hudson RHP

Born: 03/09/87   Age: 32   Bats: R   Throws: R
Height: 6'3"   Weight: 225   Origin: Round 5, 2008 Draft (#150 overall)

YEAR	TEAM	LVL	AGE	W	L	SV	G	GS	IP	H	HR	BB/9	K/9	K	GB%	BABIP
2016	ARI	MLB	29	3	2	5	70	0	60^1	65	6	3.3	8.7	58	41%	.331
2017	PIT	MLB	30	2	7	0	71	0	61^2	57	7	4.8	9.6	66	44%	.312
2018	LAN	MLB	31	3	2	0	40	1	46	38	6	3.5	8.6	44	39%	.256
2019	ANA	MLB	32	2	1	0	42	0	44^1	40	6	3.9	9.0	44	41%	.282

Breakout: 24%   Improve: 43%   Collapse: 20%   Attrition: 7%   MLB: 86%
Comparables: Tyler Yates, Santiago Casilla, Tippy Martinez

Hudson's first month of the season was filled with more ups and downs than the newest attraction at Cedar Point. Jettisoned from the Pirates to the Rays in a swap for Corey Dickerson, the righty produced an ERA halfway to his age in Spring Training and found himself wandering between baseball cities once again. The Dodgers scooped him up and Hudson tossed 46 solid, unspectacular innings. After adding a sinker to his repertoire in 2017, Hudson all but scrapped the offering this year, sticking to his trusty four-seam-slider mix. The result was an extra tick on the heater, reverse platoon splits and the best swinging strike rate since his first full year as a reliever. The 31-year-old made fewer back-to-back appearances last season, however, and potential disaster nearly struck the two-time Tommy John survivor when an inflamed elbow cut his season short in August. He'll head into 2019 with both one of the more root-forable baseball biographies to pitch to prospective employers and an arm that perhaps more closely resembles the setting of a MacGruber sketch.

YEAR	TEAM	LVL	AGE	WHIP	ERA	DRA	WARP	MPH	FB%	WHF	CSP
2016	ARI	MLB	29	1.44	5.22	5.24	-0.2	97.7	62.8	13	44.5
2017	PIT	MLB	30	1.46	4.38	4.74	0.3	96.7	60.2	12.8	47.3
2018	LAN	MLB	31	1.22	4.11	4.63	0.2	96.8	54.4	14	51.3
2019	ANA	MLB	32	1.33	4.66	4.73	0.2	96.0	58.6	13.1	47.8

Daniel Hudson, continued

Pitch Shape vs LHH

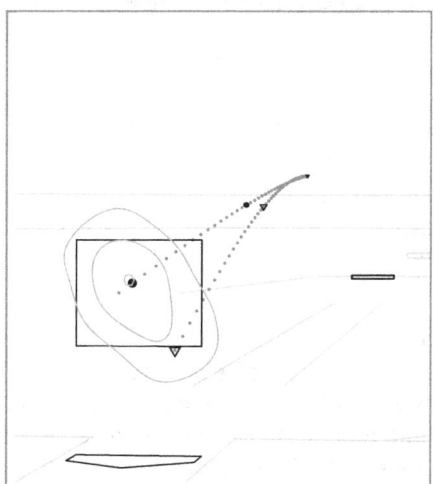

Pitch Shape vs RHH

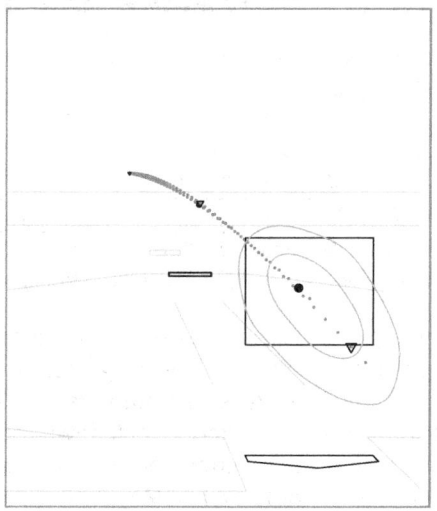

Type	Frequency	Velocity	H Movement	V Movement
● Fastball	54.4%	95.9 [111]	-5.6 [105]	-13.3 [108]
☐ Sinker				
+ Cutter				
▲ Changeup	4.6%	86.7 [105]	-14.5 [83]	-23.1 [112]
✕ Splitter				
▽ Slider	41.0%	87.1 [112]	1.7 [86]	-29.5 [110]
◇ Curveball				
⊕ Slow Curveball				
✱ Knuckleball				
▼ Screwball				

Keynan Middleton RHP
Born: 09/12/93 Age: 25 Bats: R Throws: R
Height: 6'2" Weight: 215 Origin: Round 3, 2013 Draft (#95 overall)

YEAR	TEAM	LVL	AGE	W	L	SV	G	GS	IP	H	HR	BB/9	K/9	K	GB%	BABIP
2016	INL	A+	22	1	1	0	25	0	36¹	22	7	5.0	13.9	56	34%	.227
2016	ARK	AA	22	0	0	6	13	0	15	11	1	2.4	10.8	18	42%	.270
2016	SLC	AAA	22	0	1	2	8	0	14²	14	1	2.5	8.6	14	48%	.302
2017	SLC	AAA	23	0	0	2	10	0	12²	11	0	2.8	5.7	8	36%	.282
2017	ANA	MLB	23	6	1	3	64	0	58¹	60	11	2.8	9.7	63	38%	.318
2018	ANA	MLB	24	0	0	6	16	0	17²	14	1	4.6	8.2	16	33%	.295
2019	ANA	MLB	25	2	2	0	32	0	34¹	31	5	4.6	9.5	36	38%	.291

Breakout: 33% Improve: 47% Collapse: 13% Attrition: 22% MLB: 72%
Comparables: Will Smith, Ian Krol, Logan Kensing

Middleton's a classic fastball-slider combo pitcher against righties, and he'll turn over a viable changeup against those weird lefties, so he can retire batters in a number of ways. The man they call Key was clearly the Angels' most reliable bullpen option, tasked to lock down the ninth inning. He was slotted on an All-Star track until the inexorable fragility of tendons in pitchers reached a yowling climax for Middleton last May. The hope is that Key comes back with a fresh new UCL later this year and re-assumes the closer's role by 2020.

YEAR	TEAM	LVL	AGE	WHIP	ERA	DRA	WARP	MPH	FB%	WHF	CSP
2016	INL	A+	22	1.16	3.72	1.53	1.5				
2016	ARK	AA	22	1.00	1.20	1.71	0.5				
2016	SLC	AAA	22	1.23	4.91	4.39	0.1				
2017	SLC	AAA	23	1.18	2.84	4.31	0.1				
2017	ANA	MLB	23	1.34	3.86	3.80	0.9	99.2	62.6	18.2	48.7
2018	ANA	MLB	24	1.30	2.04	5.55	-0.1	98.4	64.4	11	44.7
2019	ANA	MLB	25	1.42	4.90	4.85	0.1	98.7	64.7	16.6	47.6

Keynan Middleton, continued

Pitch Shape vs LHH

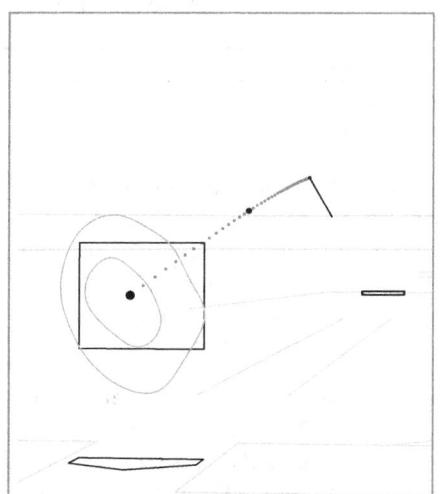

Pitch Shape vs RHH

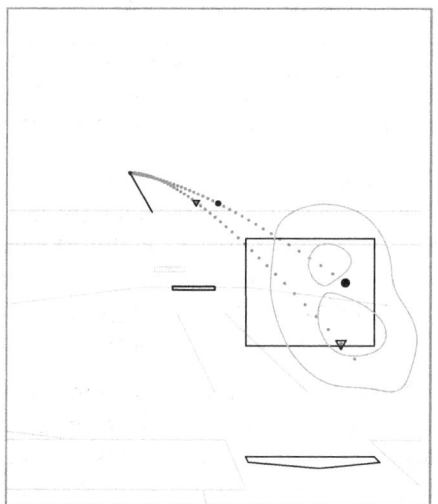

Type	Frequency	Velocity	H Movement	V Movement
● Fastball	64.4%	96.7 [114]	-7.9 [94]	-12.2 [111]
☐ Sinker				
+ Cutter				
▲ Changeup	9.4%	87.7 [109]	-15 [80]	-25.1 [107]
× Splitter				
▽ Slider	26.2%	87 [111]	2.2 [88]	-29.5 [110]
◇ Curveball				
✦ Slow Curveball				
✳ Knuckleball				
▼ Screwball				

Shohei Ohtani RHP

Born: 07/05/94 Age: 24 Bats: L Throws: R
Height: 6'4" Weight: 200 Origin: International Free Agent, 2017

YEAR	TEAM	LVL	AGE	W	L	SV	G	GS	IP	H	HR	BB/9	K/9	K	GB%	BABIP
2018	ANA	MLB	23	4	2	0	10	10	51²	38	6	3.8	11.0	63	40%	.269
2019	ANA	MLB	24	2	2	0	7	7	36	28	4	3.9	11.1	45	40%	.282

Breakout: 27%   Improve: 55%   Collapse: 12%   Attrition: 5%   MLB: 97%
Comparables: Mark Langston, Hal Newhouser, Vinegar Bend Mizell

You, a baseball fan, have various circles of connections: friends and online acquaintances who are equally zealous about the sport; co-workers and neighbors who dabble in all the athletic prowesses; and those people you love but could (possibly?) identify a baseball among a lineup of other spheres. Baseball news stories flash by our lives and depending on the magnitude/nerdery of the story, you share it with one or more of those circles.

When the Ohtani scouting report hit the states, you told everyone, even your grandparents who stopped watching baseball in 1962 when players kept hot-doggin' it. So many paragraphs have been rendered based on his substance and his phenomenon, so place this in the simplest of contexts: Ohtani is one of the league's best hitters and one of the league's best pitchers and the last person to embody both roles was Babe Ruth. And he did it simultaneously for only a couple seasons. Everyone has heard of general baseball players existing, but Ohtani, or at least the idea of him, transcends generations.

You are painfully aware that this year Thomas Edward John surgery will keep him off the mound but not from the batter's box, so we'll still get to watch him mash, at least. And a year from now you can go back to being the herald that cries the wonders of the two-way player.

YEAR	TEAM	LVL	AGE	WHIP	ERA	DRA	WARP	MPH	FB%	WHF	CSP
2018	ANA	MLB	23	1.16	3.31	3.46	1.1	99.5	46.4	15.5	47.6
2019	ANA	MLB	24	1.20	3.72	3.72	0.7	99.3	47.8	15.9	49.1

Shohei Ohtani, continued

Pitch Shape vs LHH

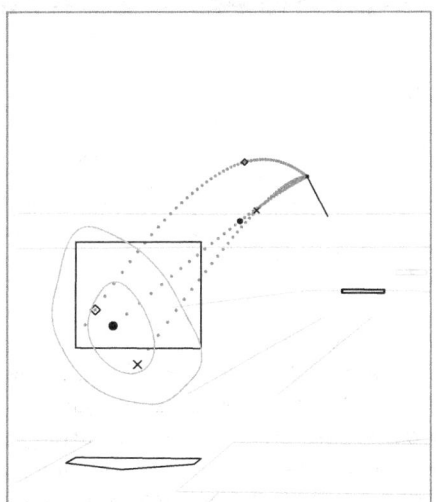

Pitch Shape vs RHH

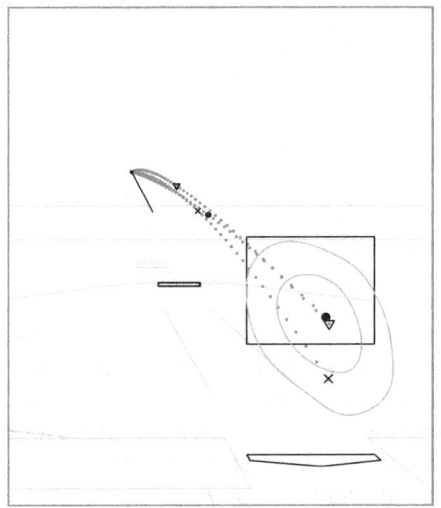

Type		Frequency	Velocity	H Movement	V Movement
●	Fastball	46.3%	97.4 [116]	-5.2 [107]	-11.7 [113]
□	Sinker	0.1%	98.4 [130]	-13.3 [95]	-12.2 [127]
+	Cutter				
▲	Changeup				
×	Splitter	22.4%	88 [113]	-4.4 [114]	-29.5 [100]
▽	Slider	24.6%	82.2 [90]	13.8 [139]	-34.8 [95]
◇	Curveball	6.6%	74.6 [86]	10.4 [111]	-58.5 [76]
⊕	Slow Curveball				
✷	Knuckleball				
▼	Screwball				

Felix Pena RHP

Born: 02/25/90   Age: 29   Bats: R   Throws: R
Height: 6'2"   Weight: 185   Origin: International Free Agent, 2009

YEAR	TEAM	LVL	AGE	W	L	SV	G	GS	IP	H	HR	BB/9	K/9	K	GB%	BABIP
2016	IOW	AAA	26	3	4	3	36	0	63^1	46	4	3.3	11.5	81	35%	.288
2016	CHN	MLB	26	0	0	1	11	0	9	5	1	3.0	13.0	13	42%	.222
2017	IOW	AAA	27	2	1	6	24	0	39	42	6	3.2	10.6	46	42%	.346
2017	CHN	MLB	27	1	0	0	25	0	34^1	35	8	4.7	9.7	37	35%	.300
2018	SLC	AAA	28	1	2	0	10	9	33^1	30	2	4.3	10.3	38	39%	.346
2018	ANA	MLB	28	3	5	0	19	17	92^2	87	12	2.7	8.3	85	44%	.288
2019	ANA	MLB	29	4	4	0	11	11	58^1	57	10	3.8	8.7	57	40%	.293

Breakout: 25%   Improve: 40%   Collapse: 21%   Attrition: 20%   MLB: 69%
Comparables: Mike Fiers, Mike Bolsinger, Tyler Lyons

The Angels executed a minor heist when they acquired Pena, an extremely forgettable reliever, from the Cubs for peace of mind, then converted him to the Church of Sinkertology. The sinker was exactly what his polished secondaries needed, and he added a changeup for good measure. He's also now a starting pitcher, a role he abandoned in the Cubs minor league system. Given the quick transformation it's tough to project his 2019 but Pena has demonstrated that he can hold his own in a major-league rotation, and it's extremely easy to project the Cubs' faces right now.

YEAR	TEAM	LVL	AGE	WHIP	ERA	DRA	WARP	MPH	FB%	WHF	CSP
2016	IOW	AAA	26	1.09	3.41	2.51	1.8				
2016	CHN	MLB	26	0.89	4.00	2.41	0.3	95.3	59.7	18.6	49.4
2017	IOW	AAA	27	1.44	5.54	2.72	1.1				
2017	CHN	MLB	27	1.54	5.24	5.46	-0.1	96.0	65.8	13.4	46.7
2018	SLC	AAA	28	1.38	3.51	4.10	0.5				
2018	ANA	MLB	28	1.24	4.18	4.15	1.2	94.1	57.9	11.8	46.2
2019	ANA	MLB	29	1.39	4.89	5.06	0.2	93.9	59.9	12.4	47.2

Felix Pena, continued

Pitch Shape vs LHH

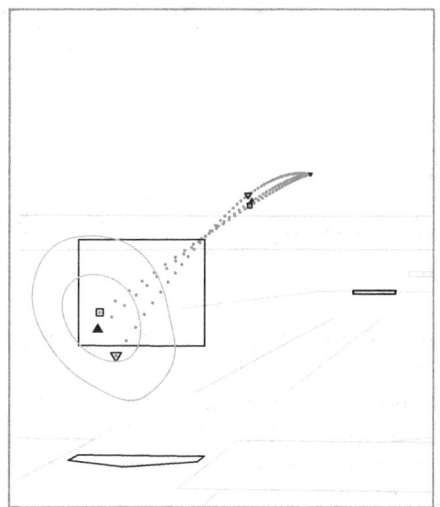

Pitch Shape vs RHH

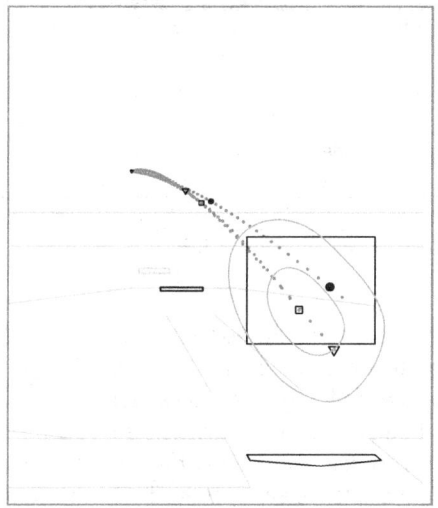

Type	Frequency	Velocity	H Movement	V Movement
● Fastball	7.2%	93.5 [103]	-7.3 [97]	-13.5 [107]
▢ Sinker	50.7%	92.7 [101]	-12.9 [98]	-17.3 [110]
+ Cutter				
▲ Changeup	7.3%	85.8 [102]	-8.5 [115]	-24.1 [109]
✕ Splitter				
▽ Slider	34.8%	82.3 [90]	6.1 [105]	-37 [88]
◇ Curveball				
⊕ Slow Curveball				
✳ Knuckleball				
▼ Screwball				

Noe Ramirez   RHP

Born: 12/22/89   Age: 29   Bats: R   Throws: R
Height: 6'3"   Weight: 195   Origin: Round 4, 2011 Draft (#142 overall)

YEAR	TEAM	LVL	AGE	W	L	SV	G	GS	IP	H	HR	BB/9	K/9	K	GB%	BABIP
2016	PAW	AAA	26	2	3	7	30	0	43^2	39	3	2.3	11.1	54	44%	.333
2016	BOS	MLB	26	0	0	0	14	0	13	16	4	5.5	10.4	15	36%	.375
2017	BOS	MLB	27	0	0	0	2	0	4^2	3	2	1.9	7.7	4	23%	.091
2017	PAW	AAA	27	3	3	5	33	0	48^2	40	7	3.0	10.5	57	35%	.284
2017	ANA	MLB	27	0	0	0	10	0	8^1	3	0	4.3	10.8	10	65%	.176
2018	ANA	MLB	28	7	5	1	69	1	83^1	75	15	3.2	10.3	95	44%	.290
2019	ANA	MLB	29	2	3	0	49	0	51	45	7	3.6	9.5	54	42%	.288

Breakout: 18%   Improve: 40%   Collapse: 16%   Attrition: 24%   MLB: 75%
Comparables: Jason Motte, Heath Bell, Brad Brach

It's not often someone throws barely 90 while striking out over a quarter of the batters they face, but that's Ramirez for you. He finally broke through with a successful major-league season thanks to his oddball arsenal. Classified as a sinker, his fastball surprisingly acts more as a swing-and-miss pitch than your textbook ground-ball offering. It's the pitch that was always red flagged as one that could be easily belted into the seats, and that's no longer happening. That and a slidery-curve both lead the way for the changeup, his true out pitch. The crafty righty can get outs in any situation, but going into 2019 he'll probably be one of the first to jog out of the bullpen.

YEAR	TEAM	LVL	AGE	WHIP	ERA	DRA	WARP	MPH	FB%	WHF	CSP
2016	PAW	AAA	26	1.15	1.85	1.93	1.5				
2016	BOS	MLB	26	1.85	6.23	5.71	-0.1	91.9	47.5	13.2	46
2017	BOS	MLB	27	0.86	3.86	9.83	-0.2	91.2	50.7	16.9	48.8
2017	PAW	AAA	27	1.15	3.51	2.63	1.4				
2017	ANA	MLB	27	0.84	2.16	3.65	0.1	91.4	25.9	14.7	42.4
2018	ANA	MLB	28	1.26	4.54	3.36	1.5	91.6	41.9	12.3	46.4
2019	ANA	MLB	29	1.28	4.31	4.39	0.4	91.0	41.6	12.7	45.7

Noe Ramirez, continued

Pitch Shape vs LHH

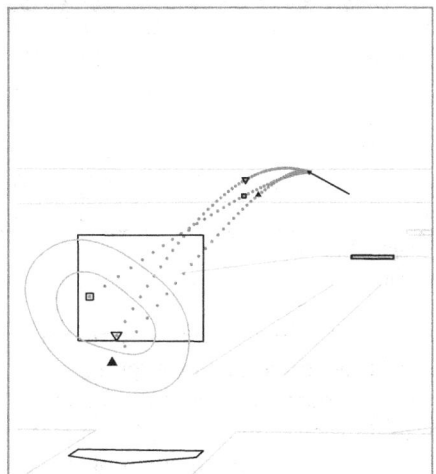

Pitch Shape vs RHH

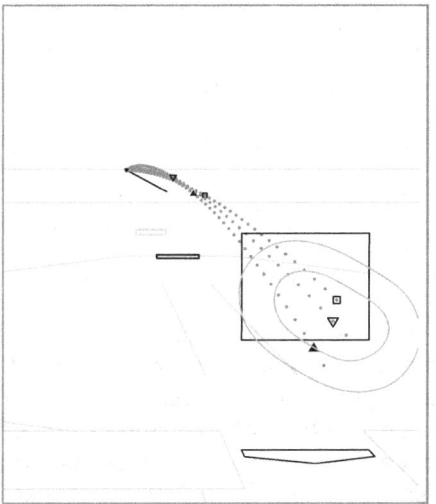

Type	Frequency	Velocity	H Movement	V Movement
● Fastball	1.7%	90.6 [94]	-9.1 [89]	-19 [90]
□ Sinker	40.3%	90.5 [90]	-9.2 [128]	-19.3 [103]
+ Cutter				
▲ Changeup	28.2%	84.9 [98]	-9.2 [111]	-38 [69]
× Splitter				
▽ Slider	29.9%	78.1 [71]	12.6 [134]	-42.1 [73]
◇ Curveball				
✦ Slow Curveball				
✻ Knuckleball				
▼ Screwball				

Hansel Robles RHP

Born: 08/13/90 Age: 28 Bats: R Throws: R
Height: 5'11" Weight: 185 Origin: International Free Agent, 2008

YEAR	TEAM	LVL	AGE	W	L	SV	G	GS	IP	H	HR	BB/9	K/9	K	GB%	BABIP
2016	NYN	MLB	25	6	4	1	68	0	77^2	69	7	4.2	9.8	85	31%	.307
2017	LVG	AAA	26	0	1	4	18	0	23^1	27	5	5.4	8.5	22	36%	.319
2017	NYN	MLB	26	7	5	0	46	0	56^2	47	10	4.6	9.5	60	35%	.259
2018	LVG	AAA	27	0	0	2	8	0	7^2	7	1	5.9	8.2	7	61%	.273
2018	NYN	MLB	27	2	2	0	16	0	19^2	21	7	4.6	10.5	23	28%	.298
2018	ANA	MLB	27	0	1	2	37	0	36^1	32	2	3.7	8.9	36	40%	.300
2019	ANA	MLB	28	2	2	0	43	0	45^2	41	7	4.4	9.2	47	37%	.284

Breakout: 25% Improve: 41% Collapse: 26% Attrition: 17% MLB: 79%
Comparables: Jensen Lewis, Shawn Tolleson, Fernando Cabrera

Robles was destined for the unrelenting journey of new uniforms in different cities. His phenomenal September put that journey on hold, however, as managers tend to like relievers that can strike out batters without giving up large quantities of home runs. He incorporated his changeup more to get him out of trouble, especially against lefties, who kept driving the ball out of town. His high-octane fastball and slider had always accelerated the fire in Flushing, which is why the Mets were more than eager to let him go on waivers. Anaheim helped him figure some things out, though, and the third pitch may be enough, given that staying in one place is the ultimate change.

YEAR	TEAM	LVL	AGE	WHIP	ERA	DRA	WARP	MPH	FB%	WHF	CSP
2016	NYN	MLB	25	1.35	3.48	4.25	0.6	98.8	63.9	12.3	49.1
2017	LVG	AAA	26	1.76	5.79	4.95	0.1				
2017	NYN	MLB	26	1.34	4.92	5.63	-0.3	97.0	66.6	9.8	48
2018	LVG	AAA	27	1.57	3.52	4.73	0.0				
2018	NYN	MLB	27	1.58	5.03	3.75	0.3	97.4	69.1	11.6	50.7
2018	ANA	MLB	27	1.29	2.97	4.90	0.0	98.6	67.5	12.5	49.5
2019	ANA	MLB	28	1.37	4.90	4.85	0.2	97.4	66.7	11.6	49.4

Hansel Robles, continued

Pitch Shape vs LHH
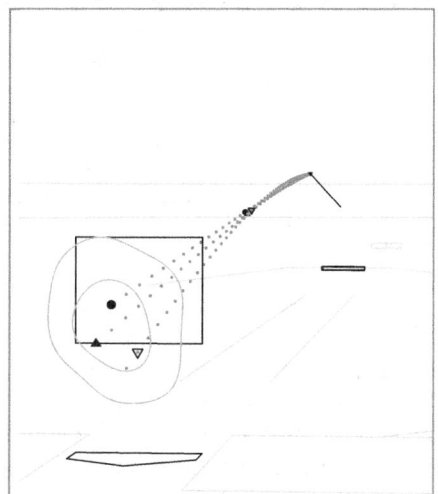

Pitch Shape vs RHH
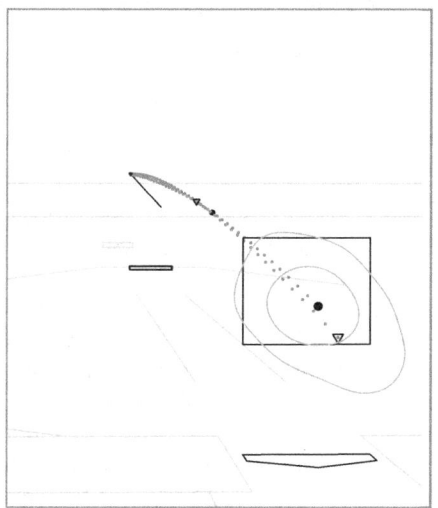

Type	Frequency	Velocity	H Movement	V Movement
● Fastball	66.8%	96.4 [112]	-11.3 [78]	-12.5 [110]
□ Sinker	1.2%	96.9 [122]	-13.5 [93]	-17.9 [108]
+ Cutter				
▲ Changeup	3.7%	91.4 [124]	-13.3 [89]	-21.6 [117]
× Splitter				
▽ Slider	28.3%	88.5 [118]	0.8 [83]	-27 [118]
◇ Curveball				
⊕ Slow Curveball				
✳ Knuckleball				
▼ Screwball				

Tyler Skaggs LHP

Born: 07/13/91   Age: 27   Bats: L   Throws: L
Height: 6'4"   Weight: 200   Origin: Round 1, 2009 Draft (#40 overall)

YEAR	TEAM	LVL	AGE	W	L	SV	G	GS	IP	H	HR	BB/9	K/9	K	GB%	BABIP
2016	SLC	AAA	24	3	2	0	7	7	32^1	19	2	2.2	12.5	45	39%	.246
2016	ANA	MLB	24	3	4	0	10	10	49^2	51	5	4.2	9.1	50	44%	.331
2017	SLC	AAA	25	0	1	0	3	3	10	14	0	5.4	6.3	7	54%	.400
2017	ANA	MLB	25	2	6	0	16	16	85	90	13	3.0	8.0	76	42%	.318
2018	ANA	MLB	26	8	10	0	24	24	125^1	127	14	2.9	9.3	129	45%	.328
2019	ANA	MLB	27	10	8	0	27	27	153	145	20	3.3	9.0	154	44%	.297

Breakout: 24%   Improve: 61%   Collapse: 18%   Attrition: 8%   MLB: 97%
Comparables: Patrick Corbin, Kevin Gausman, John Lackey

Skaggs seems to be good for a productive season every four years coinciding with the Winter Olympics, which works out since his injury status is one long event of skeleton. For a stretch he was the Angels' top starter until, yes, he missed over a month of the season, this time to an adductor muscle strain. For all the missed time, his ratios of good and bad outcomes have remained eerily constant, perhaps erring on the side of improving. He is, of course, due for his next career year in 2022, so book your hotels now.

YEAR	TEAM	LVL	AGE	WHIP	ERA	DRA	WARP	MPH	FB%	WHF	CSP
2016	SLC	AAA	24	0.84	1.67	2.54	1.0				
2016	ANA	MLB	24	1.49	4.17	5.45	-0.1	95.7	59.5	8.9	49.7
2017	SLC	AAA	25	2.00	8.10	5.40	0.0				
2017	ANA	MLB	25	1.39	4.55	5.12	0.4	94.0	60.2	8.6	45.9
2018	ANA	MLB	26	1.33	4.02	3.86	2.1	93.9	58.6	12	48.9
2019	ANA	MLB	27	1.32	4.21	4.32	2.0	93.7	59.9	10.7	48.7

Tyler Skaggs, continued

Pitch Shape vs LHH

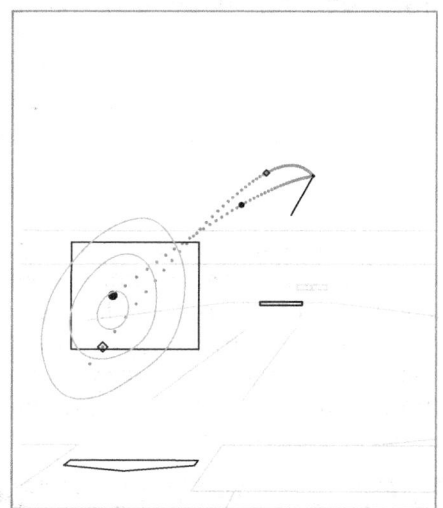

Pitch Shape vs RHH

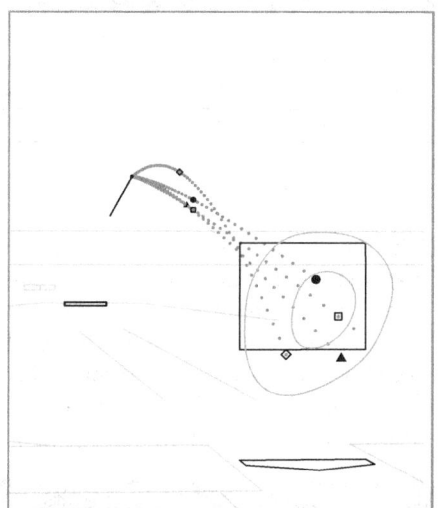

Type	Frequency	Velocity	H Movement	V Movement
● Fastball	46.2%	92.1 [99]	2.8 [118]	-13.7 [106]
□ Sinker	12.4%	91.4 [95]	12.5 [101]	-17.8 [108]
+ Cutter				
▲ Changeup	13.2%	84.7 [98]	8.3 [116]	-27.9 [98]
✕ Splitter				
▽ Slider				
◇ Curveball	28.2%	75.2 [88]	-10 [109]	-59.2 [75]
✦ Slow Curveball				
✱ Knuckleball				
▼ Screwball				

Nick Tropeano RHP

Born: 08/27/90   Age: 28   Bats: R   Throws: R
Height: 6'4"   Weight: 200   Origin: Round 5, 2011 Draft (#160 overall)

YEAR	TEAM	LVL	AGE	W	L	SV	G	GS	IP	H	HR	BB/9	K/9	K	GB%	BABIP
2016	SLC	AAA	25	1	0	0	1	1	6²	3	1	1.4	9.4	7	53%	.143
2016	ANA	MLB	25	3	2	0	13	13	68¹	70	14	4.1	9.0	68	36%	.309
2018	ANA	MLB	27	5	6	0	14	14	76	68	16	3.7	7.6	64	38%	.256
2019	ANA	MLB	28	5	6	0	16	16	84	82	14	3.9	8.3	78	38%	.288

Breakout: 23%   Improve: 56%   Collapse: 14%   Attrition: 21%   MLB: 93%
Comparables: John Maine, Wade LeBlanc, Chase Anderson

While most of the Angels pitching staff underwent the knife, because it's always smart to buy in bulk, Tropeano was the rare seraph who came *back* from Tommy John surgery and returned to his itinerant home run-donating ways. The one positive revelation was a new splitter that became an effective out pitch. His max-effort delivery produces min-effort velocity, and it remained largely good enough while it lasted. But once again he finished the year in the trainer's room, this time nursing his shoulder again. If it's not one thing, it's another.

YEAR	TEAM	LVL	AGE	WHIP	ERA	DRA	WARP	MPH	FB%	WHF	CSP
2016	SLC	AAA	25	0.60	2.70	2.51	0.2				
2016	ANA	MLB	25	1.48	3.56	5.61	-0.2	93.4	49.5	12.8	45.8
2018	ANA	MLB	27	1.30	4.74	4.78	0.5	92.0	47.5	12	45.2
2019	ANA	MLB	28	1.37	5.00	5.19	0.2	91.9	48.5	12.4	45.7

Nick Tropeano, continued

Pitch Shape vs LHH

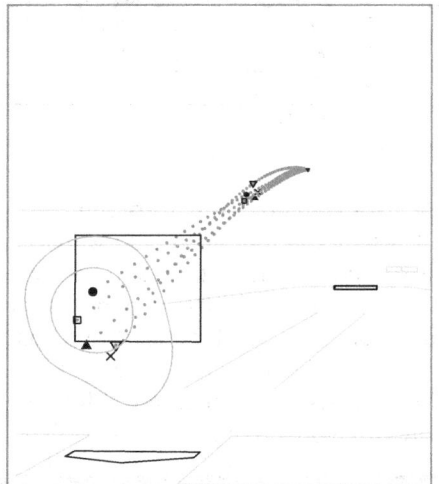

Pitch Shape vs RHH

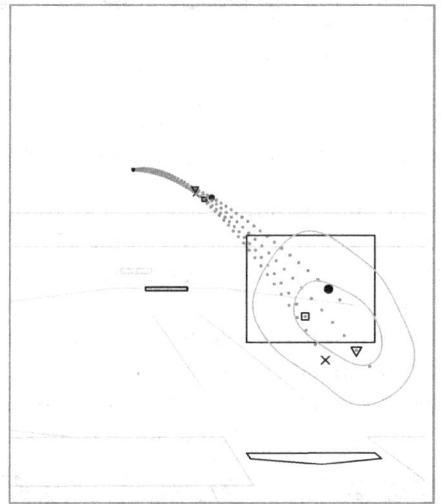

Type	Frequency	Velocity	H Movement	V Movement
● Fastball	28.1%	91.1 [95]	-11.2 [79]	-16.3 [98]
☐ Sinker	19.4%	90.5 [90]	-15.1 [79]	-20.7 [99]
+ Cutter				
▲ Changeup	13.3%	82.8 [90]	-13.5 [88]	-25.5 [105]
✕ Splitter	14.9%	82.9 [85]	-8.4 [99]	-35.6 [74]
▽ Slider	24.3%	80.2 [81]	1.9 [87]	-38 [85]
◇ Curveball				
⊕ Slow Curveball				
✱ Knuckleball				
▼ Screwball				

Los Angeles Angels 2019

Jordyn Adams CF
Born: 10/18/99   Age: 19   Bats: R   Throws: R
Height: 6'2"   Weight: 180   Origin: Round 1, 2018 Draft (#17 overall)

YEAR	TEAM	LVL	AGE	PA	R	2B	3B	HR	RBI	BB	K	SB	CS	AVG/OBP/SLG
2018	ANG	RK	18	82	8	2	2	0	5	10	23	5	2	.243/.354/.329
2018	ORM	RK	18	40	5	4	1	0	8	4	7	0	1	.314/.375/.486
2019	ANA	MLB	19	251	18	2	1	4	14	8	103	2	1	.110/.137/.177

Breakout: 5%   Improve: 7%   Collapse: 0%   Attrition: 3%   MLB: 9%
Comparables: Carlos Tocci, Engel Beltre, Franmil Reyes

Adams has a name like a pop star, the speed of a wideout, and one of the highest ceilings of anyone in the 2018 draft. A four-star football recruit with a commitment to North Carolina—where his dad is a coach—Adams showed last spring that he was more adept at the plate than many anticipated, landing him a selection in the middle of the first round. He boasts plus-plus speed, and has the bat speed and frame such that a plus power projection isn't irresponsible. Like many a high-beta prospect, Adams' future rests on the outcome of his hit tool, but if that comes around, the high notes are going to be quite something.

YEAR	TEAM	LVL	AGE	PA	DRC+	VORP	BABIP	BRR	FRAA	WARP
2018	ANG	RK	18	82	83	2.3	.362	0.9	CF(14): -4.2, RF(1): 0.0	-0.5
2018	ORM	RK	18	40	113	1.3	.379	-0.8	CF(8): 3.1	0.3
2019	ANA	MLB	19	251	-21	-26.8	.165	0.7	CF -1, RF 0	-3.0

Jo Adell CF

Born: 04/08/99 Age: 20 Bats: R Throws: R
Height: 6'3" Weight: 208 Origin: Round 1, 2017 Draft (#10 overall)

YEAR	TEAM	LVL	AGE	PA	R	2B	3B	HR	RBI	BB	K	SB	CS	AVG/OBP/SLG
2017	ANG	RK	18	132	18	6	6	4	21	10	32	5	0	.288/.351/.542
2017	ORM	RK	18	90	25	5	2	1	9	4	17	3	2	.376/.411/.518
2018	BUR	A	19	108	23	7	1	6	29	11	26	4	1	.326/.398/.611
2018	INL	A+	19	262	46	19	3	12	42	15	63	9	2	.290/.345/.546
2018	MOB	AA	19	71	14	6	0	2	6	6	22	2	0	.238/.324/.429
2019	ANA	MLB	20	251	26	8	2	9	24	9	85	3	1	.165/.195/.320

Breakout: 15%   Improve: 21%   Collapse: 0%   Attrition: 6%   MLB: 21%
Comparables: Ronald Acuna, Byron Buxton, Domingo Santana

While he didn't play the field after signing in 2017, Adell proved he was right as rain in 2018, manning center field in 69 of 99 games and scalding the ball across three different levels while firmly entrenching himself among the game's top prospects, all at the tender age of 19. His physique is enough to melt one's heart to stone, and his bat speed helps him generate prodigious power — enough to make him your first love among prospects. A-ball hurlers found that pitching to Adell was just chasing pavements, though he tired towards the end of the season, definitely not saving the best for last, as Double-A arms gave him the cold shoulder. Tepid end to the season aside, it wouldn't be crazy for you to see Adell in the majors by the end of the 2019 season, helping the Angels restore some hometown glory. What he'll be at 21 or 25? We'll leave that to the daydreamers.

YEAR	TEAM	LVL	AGE	PA	DRC+	VORP	BABIP	BRR	FRAA	WARP
2017	ANG	RK	18	132	122	13.2	.361	1.9		0.0
2017	ORM	RK	18	90	133	7.2	.463	0.4		0.3
2018	BUR	A	19	108	161	12.4	.391	1.2	CF(16): -0.4, RF(3): -0.9	0.9
2018	INL	A+	19	262	142	21.8	.345	2.0	CF(36): -5.6, RF(8): -1.1	0.7
2018	MOB	AA	19	71	99	4.5	.333	-0.3	CF(17): -1.9	-0.1
2019	ANA	MLB	20	251	36	-9.9	.208	0.4	CF -4, RF -1	-1.5

Jeremiah Jackson SS

Born: 03/26/00   Age: 19   Bats: R   Throws: R
Height: 6'0"   Weight: 165   Origin: Round 2, 2018 Draft (#57 overall)

YEAR	TEAM	LVL	AGE	PA	R	2B	3B	HR	RBI	BB	K	SB	CS	AVG/OBP/SLG
2018	ANG	RK	18	91	13	4	2	5	14	7	25	6	1	.317/.374/.598
2018	ORM	RK	18	100	13	6	3	2	9	8	34	4	1	.198/.260/.396
2019	ANA	MLB	19	251	25	6	1	9	23	2	101	3	1	.158/.164/.297

Breakout: 5%   Improve: 7%   Collapse: 0%   Attrition: 3%   MLB: 9%
Comparables: Adalberto Mondesi, Gleyber Torres, Elvis Andrus

A second-round draft pick, Jackson boasts an exciting offensive skill set for a six-spotter, and it flashed aplenty in a first professional stop in Arizona before running into resistance in the Pioneer League. Jackson's hands do the work at the plate, generating dynamic bat speed that results in impressive raw power, especially for a middle infielder. They're less reliable in the field, however, where he was error prone at shortstop despite having enough arm strength for the position. He might be a second baseman or third baseman when it is all said and done, but he has the offensive projection to justify a position switch if it comes to that.

YEAR	TEAM	LVL	AGE	PA	DRC+	VORP	BABIP	BRR	FRAA	WARP
2018	ANG	RK	18	91	150	13.9	.396	1.3	SS(21): -1.3	0.5
2018	ORM	RK	18	100	26	-1.5	.286	-0.3	SS(21): -1.7, 2B(1): 0.0	-0.7
2019	ANA	MLB	19	251	15	-15.6	.215	0.5	SS -1, 2B 0	-1.8

Jahmai Jones 2B

Born: 08/04/97 Age: 21 Bats: R Throws: R
Height: 6'0" Weight: 215 Origin: Round 2, 2015 Draft (#70 overall)

YEAR	TEAM	LVL	AGE	PA	R	2B	3B	HR	RBI	BB	K	SB	CS	AVG/OBP/SLG
2016	ORM	RK	18	226	49	12	3	3	20	21	29	19	6	.321/.404/.459
2016	BUR	A	18	70	8	1	0	1	10	5	13	1	0	.242/.294/.306
2017	BUR	A	19	387	54	18	4	9	30	32	63	18	7	.272/.338/.425
2017	INL	A+	19	191	32	11	3	5	17	13	43	9	6	.302/.368/.488
2018	INL	A+	20	347	47	10	5	8	35	43	63	13	3	.235/.338/.383
2018	MOB	AA	20	212	33	10	4	2	20	24	51	11	1	.245/.335/.375
2019	ANA	MLB	21	251	28	7	1	6	22	15	64	6	2	.196/.246/.320

Breakout: 20% Improve: 22% Collapse: 0% Attrition: 14% MLB: 22%
Comparables: Jonathan Schoop, Adrian Cardenas, Delino DeShields

Jones carried the torch for a starved Angel system over the first couple years of his career, as the club signed free agents and lost draft picks. But with an influx of talent into the system, and specifically in the outfield, Jones took on a transition to the keystone this season — a position he hadn't manned since high school. He acclimated to the role over the course of the season, but the process appeared to take a toll on his bat, as he struggled to make consistent contact at either stop. There are positives though: he walked more than ever before and his athleticism still shines. A mixed bag of a season has Jones a bit of a forgotten man in prospect circles, but it's not because he's lost any luster so much as there are finally additional stars in the Orange County sky around him.

YEAR	TEAM	LVL	AGE	PA	DRC+	VORP	BABIP	BRR	FRAA	WARP
2016	ORM	RK	18	226	145	23.1	.364	1.3	CF(41): -4.2, RF(4): -0.5	0.8
2016	BUR	A	18	70	85	-1.3	.286	0.2	CF(8): -0.7, RF(4): 1.8	0.1
2017	BUR	A	19	387	115	27.2	.309	5.7	CF(65): -3.4, LF(16): 0.5	1.5
2017	INL	A+	19	191	125	17.7	.379	2.0	CF(37): -9.7, LF(3): -0.5	-0.3
2018	INL	A+	20	347	112	12.5	.272	1.5	2B(70): -6.9	-0.1
2018	MOB	AA	20	212	104	5.7	.323	-1.5	2B(45): -1.7	-0.1
2019	ANA	MLB	21	251	47	-6.7	.238	0.7	2B -2, CF 0	-1.0

D'Shawn Knowles OF

Born: 01/16/01   Age: 18   Bats: B   Throws: R
Height: 6'0"   Weight: 165   Origin: International Free Agent, 2017

YEAR	TEAM	LVL	AGE	PA	R	2B	3B	HR	RBI	BB	K	SB	CS	AVG/OBP/SLG
2018	ANG	RK	17	130	19	4	1	1	14	15	27	7	4	.301/.385/.381
2018	ORM	RK	17	123	27	9	2	4	15	13	38	2	3	.321/.398/.550
2019	ANA	MLB	18	251	17	3	0	4	20	9	84	2	1	.157/.185/.224

Comparables: Adalberto Mondesi, Wilmer Flores, Tommy Brown

Part of the Bahamian wave of prospects (Jazz Chisholm, Lucius Fox, Trent Deveaux, Kristian Robinson, etc.), the switch-hitting Knowles stood out in his debut season. He's a small guy but the frame suggests average raw power may come in time, and his contact skills and approach impressed scouts and coaches alike. He's known for his speed, and natural feel in center field, and given the organization's penchant for pushing prospects, Knowles could see full-season ball at the tender age of 18. A competitive player with a strong work ethic, Knowles projects as a table-setting, top-of-the-order bat who should be able to remain in center for the long haul.

YEAR	TEAM	LVL	AGE	PA	DRC+	VORP	BABIP	BRR	FRAA	WARP
2018	ANG	RK	17	130	134	9.6	.384	1.1	LF(13): -3.1, CF(9): -0.5	0.0
2018	ORM	RK	17	123	123	8.6	.463	0.3	CF(17): -1.2, RF(9): 1.8	0.4
2019	ANA	MLB	18	251	3	-21.5	.216	-0.5	CF 0, RF 0	-2.4

Kevin Maitan 3B

Born: 02/12/00   Age: 19   Bats: B   Throws: R
Height: 6'2"   Weight: 190   Origin: International Free Agent, 2016

YEAR	TEAM	LVL	AGE	PA	R	2B	3B	HR	RBI	BB	K	SB	CS	AVG/OBP/SLG
2017	BRA	RK	17	37	5	3	0	0	3	2	10	1	0	.314/.351/.400
2017	DNV	RK	17	139	10	5	1	2	15	9	39	1	0	.220/.273/.323
2018	ORM	RK	18	284	42	13	1	8	26	19	66	1	2	.248/.306/.397
2019	ANA	MLB	19	251	17	4	0	7	19	1	95	0	0	.116/.119/.212

Breakout: 5%   Improve: 8%   Collapse: 0%   Attrition: 3%   MLB: 10%
Comparables: Francisco Pena, Adalberto Mondesi, Engel Beltre

The Miguel Cabrera comparisons were never fair, and they've long since faded away. Even the standard top prospect luster has been coated by the patina of stagnant development. It's fair to put a parenthetical "or lack thereof" behind that last statement, but we've long told you that development isn't linear for a reason. Maitan still has a spate of potential league-average tools, but the distance between present and projection has gotten longer and bumpier. The bat lacks polish and his inability to make consistent, hard contact makes his power play down in-game. His weight has fluctuated, and hasn't really ended up in a good place. He's already moved off of short and there's a good chance he's a first baseman when it is all said and done, and while that worked for Miggy, they call them "generational talents" for a reason.

YEAR	TEAM	LVL	AGE	PA	DRC+	VORP	BABIP	BRR	FRAA	WARP
2017	BRA	RK	17	37	102	2.0	.440	0.3	SS(5): -1.7	-0.1
2017	DNV	RK	17	139	38	0.2	.295	-0.7	SS(30): 0.9	-0.6
2018	ORM	RK	18	284	64	7.4	.303	1.1	3B(40): 3.3, SS(21): -3.1	-0.4
2019	ANA	MLB	19	251	-20	-29.8	.149	-0.5	3B 0, SS -1	-3.3

Brandon Marsh OF

Born: 12/18/97 Age: 21 Bats: L Throws: R
Height: 6'4" Weight: 210 Origin: Round 2, 2016 Draft (#60 overall)

YEAR	TEAM	LVL	AGE	PA	R	2B	3B	HR	RBI	BB	K	SB	CS	AVG/OBP/SLG
2017	ORM	RK	19	192	47	13	5	4	44	9	35	10	2	.350/.396/.548
2018	BUR	A	20	154	26	12	1	3	24	21	40	4	0	.295/.390/.470
2018	INL	A+	20	426	59	15	6	7	46	52	118	10	4	.256/.348/.385
2019	ANA	MLB	21	251	25	10	1	6	23	15	80	2	0	.203/.247/.332

Breakout: 1% Improve: 5% Collapse: 0% Attrition: 2% MLB: 5%
Comparables: Michael Saunders, Daniel Fields, Domonic Brown

Marsh put his bevy of tools on display in his first taste of full-season ball, splitting time between center and right field, and producing so well with the bat that he earned an early-season promotion to High-A Inland Empire. At 20 years old, it was an aggressive promotion, and his bat got bogged down facing the more advanced pitching of the California League. Marsh did make swing adjustments throughout the year, sacrificing some plane to keep the bat in the zone longer, and profiled as a gap-to-gap hitter who could grow into above-average home run pop by season's end. Variance swamps a lot, but one constant was Marsh's impressive approach across both levels. He's consistently posted high BABIPs throughout his brief career, but there's no reason to believe his production is inflated because of it: he has the speed and hard contact to justify it. There's a chance Marsh will have to move off center in the long term, but there's enough projection in the bat and the overall profile that he can be a regular in an outfield corner.

YEAR	TEAM	LVL	AGE	PA	DRC+	VORP	BABIP	BRR	FRAA	WARP
2017	ORM	RK	19	192	120	18.1	.417	3.2	RF(26): -1.9, CF(11): 1.5	0.7
2018	BUR	A	20	154	137	12.2	.400	2.9	CF(14): 1.2, RF(13): -1.3	1.2
2018	INL	A+	20	426	108	21.2	.356	4.3	CF(50): -0.8, RF(33): 3.0	1.1
2019	ANA	MLB	21	251	53	-6.0	.275	-0.1	CF 0, RF 0	-0.5

Shohei Ohtani DH

Born: 07/05/94   Age: 24   Bats: L   Throws: R
Height: 6'4"   Weight: 200   Origin: International Free Agent, 2017

YEAR	TEAM	LVL	AGE	PA	R	2B	3B	HR	RBI	BB	K	SB	CS	AVG/OBP/SLG
2018	ANA	MLB	23	367	59	21	2	22	61	37	102	10	4	.285/.361/.564
2019	ANA	MLB	24	349	48	17	2	17	52	35	91	5	2	.265/.344/.498

Breakout: 5%   Improve: 62%   Collapse: 4%   Attrition: 3%   MLB: 98%
Comparables: Frank Robinson, Willie McCovey, Bob Robertson

You, a baseball fan, have various circles of connections: friends and online acquaintances who are equally zealous about the sport; co-workers and neighbors who dabble in all the athletic prowesses; and those people you love but could (possibly?) identify a baseball among a lineup of other spheres. Baseball news stories flash by our lives and depending on the magnitude/nerdery of the story, you share it with one or more of those circles.

When the Ohtani scouting report hit the states, you told everyone, even your grandparents who stopped watching baseball in 1962 when players kept hot-doggin' it. So many paragraphs have been rendered based on his substance and his phenomenon, so place this in the simplest of contexts: Ohtani is one of the league's best hitters and one of the league's best pitchers and the last person to embody both roles was Babe Ruth. And he did it simultaneously for only a couple seasons. Everyone has heard of general baseball players existing, but Ohtani, or at least the idea of him, transcends generations.

You are painfully aware that this year Thomas Edward John surgery will keep him off the mound but not from the batter's box, so we'll still get to watch him mash, at least. And a year from now you can go back to being the herald that cries the wonders of the two-way player.

YEAR	TEAM	LVL	AGE	PA	DRC+	VORP	BABIP	BRR	FRAA	WARP
2018	ANA	MLB	23	367	129	23.2	.350	-2.3	P(10): 0.7	1.7
2019	ANA	MLB	24	349	124	15.7	.318	-0.1		1.7

Los Angeles Angels 2019

Luis Rengifo   INF
Born: 02/26/97   Age: 22   Bats: B   Throws: R
Height: 5'10"   Weight: 165   Origin: International Free Agent, 2013

YEAR	TEAM	LVL	AGE	PA	R	2B	3B	HR	RBI	BB	K	SB	CS	AVG/OBP/SLG
2016	MRN	RK	19	124	16	7	2	1	9	13	31	22	3	.239/.325/.367
2017	CLN	A	20	450	65	24	4	11	44	33	80	29	14	.250/.318/.413
2017	BGR	A	20	104	14	3	1	1	8	8	17	5	3	.250/.308/.333
2018	INL	A+	21	190	36	11	3	2	16	27	22	22	8	.323/.426/.466
2018	MOB	AA	21	181	37	10	5	2	21	23	22	13	2	.305/.420/.477
2018	SLC	AAA	21	219	36	9	5	3	27	25	31	6	6	.274/.358/.421
2019	ANA	MLB	22	132	17	5	2	3	13	12	25	5	2	.239/.318/.393

Breakout: 18%   Improve: 38%   Collapse: 0%   Attrition: 23%   MLB: 42%
Comparables: Ivan De Jesus, Daniel Robertson, J.P. Crawford

Rengifo didn't stay out of the AL West for long, departing the Mariners but landing in Anaheim by way of Tampa Bay. Like many of the other prospects in this system, Rengifo appeared at three levels, ravaging the High-A California League and then performing even better at Double-A, before stumbling slightly in Triple-A Salt Lake City, all at the age of 21. The switch-hitter lashed *13 triples* in 2018, en route to 50 extra-base hits. While not a powerful guy, he gets the most of his fringe-average raw power by dovetailing improved pitch selection with a contact-oriented swing. He's aggressive on the bases despite average speed, and while his raw number of stolen bases (41) might impress, he was caught 16 times on the year and was notably successful only 50 percent of the time at Triple-A. Rengifo has the traditional profile of a utility man, but his patience at the plate and newfound power could push him into a second-division starter role.

YEAR	TEAM	LVL	AGE	PA	DRC+	VORP	BABIP	BRR	FRAA	WARP
2016	MRN	RK	19	124	92	7.1	.325	3.3	3B(12): -0.5, 2B(10): 2.9	0.3
2017	CLN	A	20	450	108	22.0	.285	4.3	SS(31): -2.8, 2B(25): 2.8	1.7
2017	BGR	A	20	104	109	6.0	.295	0.4	SS(23): -1.5	0.3
2018	INL	A+	21	190	174	28.1	.365	2.5	SS(36): 3.9, 2B(2): 0.0	2.3
2018	MOB	AA	21	181	143	14.2	.346	-1.0	SS(30): -3.4, 2B(9): -0.8	0.7
2018	SLC	AAA	21	219	112	12.0	.310	3.3	2B(31): -1.5, SS(16): 0.1	1.0
2019	ANA	MLB	22	132	95	4.4	.275	0.5	SS -1, 3B 0	0.3

Matt Thaiss 1B

Born: 05/06/95 Age: 24 Bats: L Throws: R
Height: 6'0" Weight: 195 Origin: Round 1, 2016 Draft (#16 overall)

YEAR	TEAM	LVL	AGE	PA	R	2B	3B	HR	RBI	BB	K	SB	CS	AVG/OBP/SLG
2016	ORM	RK	21	71	16	7	1	2	12	4	4	2	4	.338/.394/.569
2016	BUR	A	21	226	24	12	3	4	31	22	28	1	0	.276/.351/.427
2017	INL	A+	22	385	46	13	4	8	48	40	59	4	3	.265/.353/.399
2017	MOB	AA	22	221	29	14	0	1	25	37	50	4	3	.292/.412/.388
2018	MOB	AA	23	176	24	10	2	6	25	16	35	2	1	.287/.352/.490
2018	SLC	AAA	23	400	54	24	6	10	51	28	68	6	3	.277/.328/.457
2019	ANA	MLB	24	100	11	5	1	3	11	7	23	1	0	.228/.280/.402

Breakout: 3% Improve: 14% Collapse: 0% Attrition: 14% MLB: 17%
Comparables: O'Koyea Dickson, David Cooper, Chad Wallach

Thaiss runs like a what, what, what? Okay, Sisqo wouldn't have made a useful scout. Running isn't part of Thaiss' game anyway and, concerningly, neither was power entering the 2018 season. He came out trying to change minds, sending a career-high 16 balls over the fence between two different levels. There was a tradeoff though, as Thaiss' trademark patience took a hit and his overall production relative to the league average didn't change too much despite the different shape of it. Limited to first base defensively, there's a lot of pressure on the bat. There's a good chance he's a major leaguer at some point, but he's more likely to be remembered as the guy who was taken one pick ahead of Forrest Whitley than anything else. That's okay though, Sisqo's only remembered for one thing too.

YEAR	TEAM	LVL	AGE	PA	DRC+	VORP	BABIP	BRR	FRAA	WARP
2016	ORM	RK	21	71	110	4.7	.339	-1.0	1B(15): 0.7	-0.1
2016	BUR	A	21	226	131	5.2	.302	-3.6	1B(43): 5.5	0.9
2017	INL	A+	22	385	121	13.4	.299	0.5	1B(78): 2.8	0.6
2017	MOB	AA	22	221	151	12.2	.389	-1.2	1B(46): -1.5	0.7
2018	MOB	AA	23	176	123	9.0	.331	-1.1	1B(36): 2.6	0.5
2018	SLC	AAA	23	400	94	-0.6	.314	0.2	1B(77): 5.4	0.3
2019	ANA	MLB	24	100	87	0.3	.269	-0.1	1B 1	0.1

Jeremy Beasley RHP

Born: 11/20/95 Age: 23 Bats: R Throws: R
Height: 6'3" Weight: 215 Origin: Round 30, 2017 Draft (#895 overall)

YEAR	TEAM	LVL	AGE	W	L	SV	G	GS	IP	H	HR	BB/9	K/9	K	GB%	BABIP
2017	ORM	RK	21	2	1	1	13	0	26	21	3	4.2	10.7	31	48%	.290
2018	BUR	A	22	0	2	0	6	5	23	16	0	2.7	7.4	19	40%	.254
2018	INL	A+	22	3	2	1	9	6	44^1	48	4	2.2	9.7	48	42%	.358
2018	MOB	AA	22	3	3	0	10	7	44^1	32	3	2.8	7.5	37	44%	.248
2019	ANA	MLB	23	4	4	1	38	9	76^1	74	15	4.5	8.1	69	41%	.282

Breakout: 4% Improve: 8% Collapse: 5% Attrition: 6% MLB: 15%
Comparables: Jose Quintana, P.J. Walters, Tanner Roark

It's not easy to find value in the 30th round, but the Angels just might have pulled it off. Selected in 2017, Beasley mowed down hitters across three levels, turning in a composite 2.66 ERA. His stuff won't wow you, but he can fill up the zone with his low-90s fastball(s) and bevy of offspeed offerings. He was mostly a starter this past year, but his future is likely in the bullpen, where his pedestrian offerings won't get exposed over extended outings. No matter what role Beasley embodies, that he's already seen success in Double-A can be seen as a victory given his draft status.

YEAR	TEAM	LVL	AGE	WHIP	ERA	DRA	WARP	MPH	FB%	WHF	CSP
2017	ORM	RK	21	1.27	3.12	3.04	0.7				
2018	BUR	A	22	1.00	2.35	3.68	0.4				
2018	INL	A+	22	1.33	3.05	4.67	0.3				
2018	MOB	AA	22	1.04	2.44	4.61	0.3				
2019	ANA	MLB	23	1.47	5.72	5.88	-0.8				

Griffin Canning RHP

Born: 05/11/96 Age: 23 Bats: R Throws: R
Height: 6'1" Weight: 170 Origin: Round 2, 2017 Draft (#47 overall)

YEAR	TEAM	LVL	AGE	W	L	SV	G	GS	IP	H	HR	BB/9	K/9	K	GB%	BABIP
2018	INL	A+	22	0	0	0	2	2	8²	4	0	3.1	12.5	12	56%	.222
2018	MOB	AA	22	1	0	0	10	10	45²	27	2	3.7	9.7	49	48%	.229
2018	SLC	AAA	22	3	3	0	13	13	59	68	6	3.4	9.8	64	42%	.376
2019	ANA	MLB	23	2	1	0	5	5	25	23	3	3.6	9.1	25	42%	.291

Breakout: 18% Improve: 27% Collapse: 16% Attrition: 29% MLB: 52%
Comparables: Zack Wheeler, Stephen Gonsalves, Chad Bettis

A second-round pick in 2017, Canning fell due to health concerns, and seemed to validate them as he sat out the remainder of the summer. The rest seems to have done him right, as he mowed down batters across three different levels in 2018, ending the year on the precipice of the major leagues. He attacks hitters with a four-pitch mix headlined by a fastball that saw a velo jump and regularly hit 95 mph in 2018. The heater can be flat, though, and upper-level hitters took advantage of it, as his ground ball percentage decreased with each step up the organizational ladder. He'll flash a plus slider, along with an average curve and change to round out his arsenal. Canning looks like a steal based on his draft position and could find himself in the middle of the rotation sooner rather than later. He isn't the biggest guy, though, and paired with his command concerns the whispers of a bullpen future still persist.

YEAR	TEAM	LVL	AGE	WHIP	ERA	DRA	WARP	MPH	FB%	WHF	CSP
2018	INL	A+	22	0.81	0.00	0.79	0.5				
2018	MOB	AA	22	1.01	1.97	3.86	0.8				
2018	SLC	AAA	22	1.53	5.49	3.95	1.1				
2019	ANA	MLB	23	1.28	4.18	4.29	0.3				

Patrick Sandoval   LHP

Born: 10/18/96   Age: 22   Bats: L   Throws: L
Height: 6'3"   Weight: 190   Origin: Round 11, 2015 Draft (#319 overall)

YEAR	TEAM	LVL	AGE	W	L	SV	G	GS	IP	H	HR	BB/9	K/9	K	GB%	BABIP
2016	GRV	RK	19	2	3	0	13	8	52^2	53	4	4.3	8.7	51	48%	.331
2017	TCV	A-	20	1	1	0	4	4	19	19	0	2.8	13.3	28	47%	.404
2017	QUD	A	20	2	2	1	9	7	40	38	1	3.6	10.8	48	48%	.333
2018	QUD	A	21	7	1	1	14	10	65	58	4	1.5	9.8	71	48%	.305
2018	BCA	A+	21	2	0	1	5	3	23	12	1	1.6	10.2	26	46%	.216
2018	INL	A+	21	1	0	0	3	3	14^2	6	0	3.7	12.9	21	47%	.200
2018	MOB	AA	21	1	0	0	4	4	19^2	12	0	3.7	12.4	27	40%	.286
2019	ANA	MLB	22	5	5	1	31	14	87^1	81	13	4.5	9.1	88	42%	.290

Breakout: 19%   Improve: 27%   Collapse: 6%   Attrition: 16%   MLB: 38%
Comparables: Jay Jackson, Anibal Sanchez, Gerrit Cole

Another Angels prospect who played at three different levels in 2018, Sandoval differentiated himself by also playing for five different teams. The lefty played most of the season at Low-A Quad Cities in Houston before receiving a promotion to High-A. He was then traded from Houston to Los Angeles for Martin Maldonado, and received another in-season promotion shortly after to Double-A Mobile. Sandoval attacks hitters with a straight over-the-top motion, limiting the damage right-handed batters can do to him. You might imagine Sandoval can get a lot of downer action on his curveball from that release point, and you'd be right, as the pitch flashes plus and is currently above-average. He's got a great pitcher's frame and can run his fastball into the lower-90s. Originally an overslot 11th-rounder, Sandoval projects as a backend starter or, more likely, an effective reliever.

YEAR	TEAM	LVL	AGE	WHIP	ERA	DRA	WARP	MPH	FB%	WHF	CSP
2016	GRV	RK	19	1.48	5.30	3.53	1.2				
2017	TCV	A-	20	1.32	3.79	2.83	0.5				
2017	QUD	A	20	1.35	3.83	3.29	0.9				
2018	QUD	A	21	1.06	2.49	3.25	1.4				
2018	BCA	A+	21	0.70	2.74	2.78	0.7				
2018	INL	A+	21	0.82	0.00	2.59	0.5				
2018	MOB	AA	21	1.02	1.37	2.48	0.7				
2019	ANA	MLB	22	1.42	4.91	4.99	0.4				

Jose Soriano RHP

Born: 10/20/98 Age: 20 Bats: R Throws: R
Height: 6'3" Weight: 168 Origin: International Free Agent, 2016

YEAR	TEAM	LVL	AGE	W	L	SV	G	GS	IP	H	HR	BB/9	K/9	K	GB%	BABIP
2016	DAN	RK	17	3	5	0	14	14	57	37	2	4.7	7.1	45	53%	.230
2017	ANG	RK	18	2	2	0	12	10	49	43	2	2.6	6.8	37	57%	.281
2018	BUR	A	19	1	6	0	14	14	46[1]	34	1	6.8	8.2	42	45%	.284
2019	ANA	MLB	20	2	4	0	9	9	35[1]	37	6	8.4	7.2	28	45%	.289

Comparables: Drew Hutchison, Chris Flexen, Tyler Chatwood

Soriano is one of those "don't trust the stat line" guys. He walked 35 batters in just over 46 innings in his first taste of full season ball and paired it with an ERA in the mid-fours. It's not what you want. Still, he's just 19 years old and has a highly projectable frame. He's gone from throwing in the upper-80s/low-90s when he was signed to sitting ~94 miles per hour and touching higher in Low-A. He throws both a four-seamer and a two-seamer, and both of them have a lot of life, while his secondaries flash above-average or better but have the inconsistency you'd expect out of a Low-A arm. The curve is ahead of the changeup on raw stuff; the power breaker is a bat-misser that he's willing to back-foot to left-handed batters, while the change shows the same tail as the two-seamer, but arrives a little firm in the mid-80s. Soriano is one of the better arms you haven't heard much about, and while projection is always fraught with risk, the payoff here is a potential mid-rotation stalwart.

YEAR	TEAM	LVL	AGE	WHIP	ERA	DRA	WARP	MPH	FB%	WHF	CSP
2016	DAN	RK	17	1.18	1.58	4.96	0.5				
2017	ANG	RK	18	1.16	2.94	4.12	1.0				
2018	BUR	A	19	1.49	4.47	4.21	0.5				
2019	ANA	MLB	20	1.96	7.18	7.44	-0.8				

Jose Suarez LHP

Born: 01/03/98   Age: 21   Bats: L   Throws: L
Height: 5'10"   Weight: 170   Origin: International Free Agent, 2014

YEAR	TEAM	LVL	AGE	W	L	SV	G	GS	IP	H	HR	BB/9	K/9	K	GB%	BABIP
2016	ANG	RK	18	1	3	0	11	5	40^1	48	1	2.9	10.3	46	42%	.395
2017	ANG	RK	19	1	0	0	3	3	14	10	1	2.6	12.2	19	40%	.310
2017	BUR	A	19	5	1	0	12	12	54^2	49	7	3.0	11.7	71	48%	.333
2018	INL	A+	20	0	1	0	2	2	9	6	0	1.0	18.0	18	67%	.400
2018	MOB	AA	20	2	1	0	7	7	29^2	34	0	2.4	15.5	51	37%	.500
2018	SLC	AAA	20	1	4	0	17	17	78^1	81	5	4.0	8.4	73	48%	.336
2019	ANA	MLB	21	2	1	0	14	3	26	24	4	4.3	10.0	29	42%	.295

Breakout: 15%   Improve: 20%   Collapse: 9%   Attrition: 22%   MLB: 33%
Comparables: Shelby Miller, Jake McGee, Robert Stephenson

Say it with me now: Suarez pitched at [everyone chimes in] "three different levels" this year. The stocky southpaw has the potential for three above-average pitches in his fastball, changeup, and curveball. The former two flash plus while the curve is less consistent at present. The heater has multiple looks to it with cut, run and tail, and he'll touch the mid-90s, while sitting a tick below. Suarez is shorter than scouts prefer for a starting pitcher, and he's thick through the middle, so conditioning will be important. Still, he generates good extension and plane despite his smaller stature. He repeats his mechanics well, allowing for above-average command and control — enabling his stuff to play up. He's got a middle-of-the-rotation profile if his frame can handle the innings workload (increasingly less of a problem in today's five-and-dive game).

YEAR	TEAM	LVL	AGE	WHIP	ERA	DRA	WARP	MPH	FB%	WHF	CSP
2016	ANG	RK	18	1.51	5.36	2.91	1.2				
2017	ANG	RK	19	1.00	1.93	2.02	0.6				
2017	BUR	A	19	1.23	3.62	2.85	1.6				
2018	INL	A+	20	0.78	2.00	0.89	0.5				
2018	MOB	AA	20	1.42	3.03	2.56	1.0				
2018	SLC	AAA	20	1.48	4.48	4.44	1.0				
2019	ANA	MLB	21	1.37	4.56	4.64	0.2				

LINEOUTS

Hitters

HITTER	POS	TEAM	LVL	AGE	PA	R	2B	3B	HR	RBI	BB	K	SB	CS	AVG/OBP/SLG	DRC+	WARP
Peter Bourjos	CF	GWN	AAA	31	105	16	6	5	2	9	10	19	1	0	.277/.352/.511	104	0.3
	CF	ATL	MLB	31	47	5	2	1	1	4	2	15	0	0	.205/.239/.364	63	-0.1
	CF	SAC	AAA	31	173	20	7	4	2	14	7	35	0	2	.296/.335/.426	88	0.2
Jose Briceno	C	SLC	AAA	25	118	22	5	0	8	25	4	22	3	0	.277/.297/.536	104	0.4
	C	ANA	MLB	25	128	12	2	0	5	10	8	35	0	1	.239/.299/.385	86	0.4
Kaleb Cowart	SS	SLC	AAA	26	279	36	20	3	6	45	18	52	8	1	.287/.333/.457	92	-0.2
	SS	ANA	MLB	26	124	7	7	1	1	10	10	44	1	0	.134/.210/.241	51	-0.2
Trent Deveaux	CF	ANG	Rk	18	194	20	5	0	1	11	24	68	7	4	.199/.309/.247	65	-1.0
William English	DH	ANG	Rk	17	117	13	4	0	0	8	11	34	4	0	.220/.325/.260	83	-0.3
Dustin Garneau	C	NAS	AAA	30	80	8	3	0	2	9	5	10	0	0	.208/.263/.333	68	-0.4
	C	CHA	MLB	30	3	0	0	0	0	1	1	0	0	0	.500/.667/.500	98	0.0
	C	CHR	AAA	30	160	19	9	0	7	22	16	38	0	2	.252/.340/.468	113	0.5
Livan Soto	SS	ORM	Rk	18	200	31	10	0	0	11	24	24	9	3	.291/.385/.349	110	0.8
Jared Walsh	RF	INL	A+	24	178	28	8	1	13	36	24	50	0	1	.275/.365/.604	167	1.0
	RF	MOB	AA	24	173	26	13	0	8	26	21	48	1	0	.289/.382/.537	128	0.5
	RF	SLC	AAA	24	198	32	13	0	8	37	16	56	0	0	.270/.333/.478	115	-0.1

Still a handy pinch-runner and defensive sub for September contenders, **Peter Bourjos** was stranded in Sacramento when the Giants waved the white flag. ⓧ **Jose Briceno** is proof the best catching prospects shine thanks to their hitting, but scads more will surface due to persistence. His skill shines brightest when he squats, wiggles his fingers, and snatches extra strikes. (The description of what a catcher does on a daily basis is probably why they don't advertise for catchers on CareerBuilder.) ⓧ Fielding yeoman **Kaleb Cowart** is a decent utility option, since nowhere in this rulebook does it say the DH has to bat for the pitc— never mind, found it. ⓧ One of the hotter under-the-radar names out there, Bahamian speedster **Trent Deveaux** was training with the Olympic sprinting team before signing with the Angels. He's going to be a project but has a monster top-end outcome. ⓧ Is it possible the Angels have a type? Overslot fifth-rounder **William English** was selected as a two-way player, and was the youngest player in the 2018 draft. ⓧ There's not much of a ceiling for 31-year-old infielder **Jose Fernandez**, but he sports a bit of power, which helped him reach the big leagues after his tumultuous journey from Cuba. ⓧ The ocean waves beat endlessly on the rocks, but the rocks do not move. So it is with **Dustin Garneau**, professional baseball player, catcher, human edifice. ⓧ **Jefry Marte** is a corner infielder and former ranked prospect who slowly but surely earned major-league playing time because he could hit lefties and hit with power. Fortunately for the lefties, they have figured out how to pitch to him, so he crossed the ocean to find some unfamiliarity in the NPB. ⓧ **Alex Ramirez**, a toolsy Venezuelan outfielder known

Los Angeles Angels 2019

for his raw power, was the club's top J2 signing in 2018. If he falls short of his major league dreams, the NPB might answer his calls. ⓧ If **Ryan Schimpf** retired tomorrow, we would replace him, the game would go on; in three years it would make no difference whatsoever. ⓧ One of the players stripped from the Braves, **Livan Soto** performed well in his first year with the Angels at short-season Orem. The shortstop prospect has great barrel control and defensive instincts, but generic-paper-towel strength. ⓧ We don't generally give 25-year-olds beating up on younger competition much ink, but when it's a 39th-rounder like **Jared Walsh**, we can make an exception. The 2015 selection cruised through three levels with power and patience, and ohbytheway he struck out 7 in 5 2/3 innings on the mound. ⓧ For the first time in four years, **Chris Young** The Outfielder did not appear on a baseball team that lost the first round of their postseason. Given his dimming production, it's safe to say that he will not begin another streak.

Pitchers

PITCHER	TEAM	LVL	AGE	W	L	SV	G	GS	IP	H	HR	BB/9	K/9	K	GB%	WHIP	ERA	DRA	WARP
Miguel Almonte	SLC	AAA	25	1	1	0	25	0	20^1	34	4	6.6	9.7	22	57%	2.41	10.18	6.43	-0.3
	ANA	MLB	25	0	0	0	8	0	7	9	1	3.9	9.0	7	44%	1.71	10.29	4.09	0.1
Jesus Castillo	MOB	AA	22	9	5	0	21	20	98^1	97	7	2.8	5.5	60	47%	1.30	4.94	4.75	0.7
John Curtiss	ROC	AAA	25	2	4	10	38	1	55^1	41	3	5.0	9.9	61	40%	1.30	2.77	2.79	1.5
	MIN	MLB	25	0	1	0	8	0	6^1	8	0	5.7	9.9	7	10%	1.89	5.68	5.29	0.0
Dan Jennings	MIL	MLB	31	4	5	1	72	1	64^1	66	6	3.2	6.3	45	56%	1.38	3.22	4.93	0.0
Williams Jerez	PAW	AAA	26	2	1	5	34	0	52	48	6	4.2	11.9	69	47%	1.38	3.63	3.87	0.8
	ANA	MLB	26	0	0	0	17	0	15	17	3	4.8	9.0	15	38%	1.67	6.00	5.94	-0.2
Jake Jewell	MOB	AA	25	1	0	2	7	0	13	15	1	1.4	7.6	11	73%	1.31	2.08	6.16	-0.2
	SLC	AAA	25	2	4	3	19	0	25	23	2	6.1	8.6	24	56%	1.60	3.60	5.49	-0.1
	ANA	MLB	25	0	1	0	3	0	2	2	0	4.5	4.5	1	43%	1.50	9.00	10.28	-0.1
Luis Madero	BUR	A	21	2	7	0	14	14	61^1	69	5	2.2	7.2	49	46%	1.37	4.26	4.03	0.9
	INL	A+	21	2	1	0	9	9	44^1	41	3	2.4	9.3	46	40%	1.20	2.44	3.06	1.2
Dillon Peters	MIA	MLB	25	2	2	0	7	5	27^2	34	4	4.9	5.5	17	45%	1.77	7.16	5.69	-0.1
	NWO	AAA	25	6	7	0	19	19	102^2	129	15	2.5	7.5	85	46%	1.54	5.61	3.93	1.9
J.C. Ramirez	ANA	MLB	29	0	2	0	2	2	6^2	7	3	9.4	5.4	4	23%	2.10	9.45	8.57	-0.3

As a prospect, **Miguel Almonte's** calling card was a double-plus changeup. If he's not careful, his calling card as a pro will be a double-digit ERA. ⓧ Unless **Jesus Castillo** can add velocity by filling out his wiry frame, it is difficult to imagine he is long for the rotation. If a shift to the bullpen doesn't add a little spice to his repertoire, then he might not be long for the high minors, either. ⓧ Old-school #flow and a lovely fastball won't be enough to keep **John Curtiss** in a big-League bullpen, unless he much improves the command of his slider. ⓫ The Angels accomplished something with **Oliver Drake** that no other team managed to do in 2018: clear him through waivers. ⓫ Third-round selection **Aaron Hernandez** boasts a fastball that can touch the upper 90s with sink and flashes a biting slider. Refining the consistency of his secondaries and command will determine if he can stick in the rotation. ⓫ Sparkling new Opener, available at The Leftorium! Acquire **Dan Jennings** now to record your first out! ⓫ **Williams Jerez** will long (partially) answer the question of who was sent to Anaheim in return for Ian Kinsler and (fully) answer the question of who is the most "attorneys general" player of all time. ⓫ **Jake Jewell** made his major-league debut in 2018 but a gruesome injury suffered covering home plate caused the experience to lose most of its luster. ⓫ If Wooderson got his act together and could throw a fastball, you would have **John Lamb**. The ultimate finesse pitcher underwent his second Tommy John surgery, so he really will get older while the batters stay the same age. ⓫ Acquired from the Diamondbacks in 2017 for David Hernandez, **Luis Madero** saw his stuff and strikeout rate tick up in the second half of the season, finishing strong at High-A. ⓫ Very few active pitchers strike out every fourth batter and walk every seventh. Those who do make their mark in the bullpen. **Alex Meyer** is the lone exception that still boasts a starter profile, thanks to high-velocity stuff and increased use of a sinking fastball that keeps the ball in the infield. He's also the only one with an excused absence from the 2018 season. ⓫ At 5-foot-9, Peters is the shortest pitcher on the Angels' 40-man roster, depending on how strong David Fletcher's posture is on a given day. If he had been born a righty, there's a chance he doesn't even approach the sport of baseball. ⓫ **J.C. Ramirez** doubled down on science healing his partially torn UCL. Physiology rolled snake eyes, so it was Tommy John surgery for the high-velocity, weak-contact hurler. He'll likely be tardy to 2019 as well. ⓫ The extremely shareable flamethrower **Blake Wood** had the April of his life, followed promptly by the most recent UCL replacement surgery of his life.

Angels Prospects

The State of the System:
It's not the deepest system in the world, but we are on two straight years now of it being an okay system, and man does that feel weird to type.

The Top Ten:

1 **Jo Adell   OF**   OFP: 70   Likely: 60   ETA: 2020
Born: 04/08/99   Age: 20   Bats: R   Throws: R   Height: 6'3"   Weight: 208
Origin: Round 1, 2017 Draft (#10 overall)

The Report: I've been doing this for eight seasons now. I've watched and evaluated and ranked a lot of prospects. I've got a feel for my strengths and weaknesses, my predilections and preferences. But I haven't quite figured out the secret sauce for how and why I go gonzo over a prospect. This isn't just about being a "good" prospect, a high upside guy, big stuff. I enjoyed my time watching Andrew Benintendi in Double-A. I ranked him as the third best prospect in baseball because I thought it was appropriate. It was dispassionate, academic.

Jo Adell will rank in that general area on our 2019 Top 101. Nothing that follows will be nearly as antiseptic as above.

He's built like an NFL wideout. The ball jumps off his bat. It makes *that* sound. Then it makes another sound. You can't hear it—perhaps because sound doesn't travel in the vacuum of space—but I can only assume it's the secondary thrusters going off. It. Just. Looks. Right. He's 4.2 down the line at a level of effort that would get angry diatribes written by men with graying goatees about Manny Machado. His batting practice sessions justify every watery, obviously shaken Manhattan I've had in an Appy League hotel bar. Watching Jo Adell play baseball is like watching a true virtuoso handle Tchaikovsky's Piano Concerto #1. All the movements look simple enough, familiar enough, but somehow foreign, impossible. Just remember that there is no cheering in the press box. He is not the best prospect I've ever seen, but that doesn't really matter to me. He's a very, very good one. Jo Adell is an argument for style points, for the Russian judge on presentation, and yes *sigh* even for #rig.

"The answer is dreams. Dreaming on and on. Entering the world of dreams and never coming out. Living in dreams for the rest of time." — Haruki Murakami, Sputnik Sweetheart

The Risks: Medium. Well, he struggled a little at Double-A at 19 while battling minor injuries. Past that…

Ben Carsley's Fantasy Take: You can stop asking us who the next Ronald Acuna or Juan Soto is; it's Adell, who's got such obvious upside that even the most consistent prospect doubters among us can't quibble with it. All the ingredients are here for a true, five-tool, eff-you OF1 who routinely challenges for 20/20 and maybe even 30/30 in his best years. It's always tricky throwing fantasy comps on guys like this—maybe 85% of Mookie Betts, or prime Grady Sizemore, or George Springer with 15 more steals?—because in the end, they're all special, unique fantasy unicorns. He'll likely be the top dynasty prospect in the game a year from now, and if he's not it'll more likely be because he exhausted eligibility than because anyone passed him. Craig was right.

2. Griffin Canning   RHP

OFP: 60   Likely: 50   ETA: 2019
Born: 05/11/96   Age: 23   Bats: R   Throws: R   Height: 6'1"   Weight: 170
Origin: Round 2, 2017 Draft (#47 overall)

The Report: Canning brushed aside most of the concerns about the health of his arm in 2018, blitzing through three levels of the minors and leaving a trail of Ks in his wake. He might bear a passing resemblance to the cavalcade of averagish-stuff starters we have discussed so far this year, but he's a rarer avis—the above-averagish-stuff starter. Canning is wildly advanced with four present average or better offerings. He's comfortable throwing any of them for strikes at any time, in any count.

The fastball features only average velocity but his plus command of the pitch makes it play up. He has a big 12-6 curve from his hitchy, overhead slot that has consistent shape and deception. It plays well off a tighter, shorter slider that comes out like the fastball but with sharp late tilt. The change only has average fade but he sells it well. Canning is a more-than-the-sum-of-his-parts arm, but all those parts are also above-average.

I wrote that Canning brushed aside most of the concerns about his health. His workload was tightly monitored in 2018, and he only threw ~100 innings across 25 starts. So whether or not he can handle a full starter's workload is still an open question. It's the last one here though.

The Risks: Medium. The stuff is ready; we'll see if the arm is too.

Ben Carsley's Fantasy Take: See all that stuff about how Canning has more upside than the majority of starters we've covered to this point? That means you should go all in. It feels to me as though the Dynasty Prospect Industrial Complex does not fully appreciate Canning yet; in fact, in shallower leagues that roster only 100-or-so prospects, I'd say there's a good chance he's not even owned. You should fix that, as Canning has all the ingredients of a fantasy SP4 or 5, especially playing in that cavernous park. Yes, he might get hurt, but you could also get hit by a meteor tomorrow, so let's not dwell on the bad things that could happen.

3 | **Jahmai Jones 2B** | OFP: 60 Likely: 50 ETA: 2020
Born: 08/04/97 Age: 21 Bats: R Throws: R Height: 6'0" Weight: 215
Origin: Round 2, 2015 Draft (#70 overall)

The Report: Absolutely nothing has changed for Jones in terms of the physicality, work ethic, or underlying tools over the past year. He was and is an impressive specimen, with present and projectable strength throughout his frame. It's a powerful swing, though it'll still get stiff at launch and fall into rotational movement when he gets vertical and stuck on his back side. He transfers compact and short into the zone, and impressive wrist strength tracks a quick bat to the point of contact. The barrel delivery can be uneven, but it projects to become better, and he has solid-average power that's there for the gettin' to. The defensive conversion from center to second has gone okay. Not great and immediate, but steady and progressive. He's got plenty of body control and quickness to pull it off, and the arm is accurate and strong enough to work up the middle or on the turn.

The Risks: The defensive change pushed his development back a bit, and there were times in the first half where the offense looked to suffer for the split attention. He's a higher-probability prospect than most, and he still shows outstanding effort and focus on the field. The tools speak for themselves. There might be a smidge more uncertainty to the outcome than there was a year ago, but not much.

Ben Carsley's Fantasy Take: I'm in the camp that doesn't see any fantasy star upside with Jones, but that doesn't mean he can't be useful for our purposes. For example, consider that D.J. LeMahieu hit .276 with 15 homers and 6 steals last season and was a top-20 fantasy option at the position, per ESPN's player rater. That type of contribution would seem to be Jones' floor once he's established (and likely undersells his speed), and he could end up with more of a Cesar Hernandez-esque top-15 finish as a .270 hitter who can challenge for 15 bombs and steals each. His probability and ETA are good enough to keep Jones on the 101.

4 | **Brandon Marsh OF** | OFP: 60 Likely: 50 ETA: 2020
Born: 12/18/97 Age: 21 Bats: L Throws: R Height: 6'4" Weight: 210
Origin: Round 2, 2016 Draft (#60 overall)

The Report: When the 20-year-old Marsh arrived at Inland Empire mid-summer, his load generally looked mechanical and uncertain, which led to imbalanced swings that lacked extension. From there though, he made adjustments to incorporate his lower half better and control the outer part of the plate, and things started to click. His approach is patient but appropriately aggressive in context, he hangs in pretty well against lefties, and he creates good torque to bring plenty of natural strength into his swings. There's plus power in the tank, but the game version'll probably top out at average without a significant mechanical overhaul.

Marsh is an excellent athlete with advanced control of his Jim Mackey-framed levers, and there's plus speed that should stay at least above-average through maturity. He leverages plus arm strength with high-effort throws that track well and hold line. He goes and gets it in center as well as anyone the system has produced in recent years, but can hold down right just as easily, thanks to a strong arm and good reads off the bat.

The Risks: Moderate. He's been pushed quickly, and the combination of raw offensive skills and aggressive promotions means we're projecting more development than usual for a High-A guy. The high-end strength and athleticism gives him a lot to work with, however, and his demonstrated ability to make in-season adjustments points to a higher-likelihood prospect.

Ben Carsley's Fantasy Take: I think Marsh often gets oversold as a super high-upside fantasy outfielder because of his natural raw power. That's likely a mistake—there is no future OF1 upside here—but Marsh could be plenty useful as a fantasy OF3/4 who's more of a pure OF3 in OBP leagues. Overall, I see some Aaron Hicks potential in Marsh's future as a guy who does enough in the power and speed categories to mitigate a mediocre (but certainly tolerable) average. We'll just hope that, unlike with Hicks, it doesn't take Marsh like five years to reach that modest but meaningful ceiling.

5

Jordyn Adams OF   OFP: 60   Likely: 50   ETA: 2022
Born: 10/18/99   Age: 19   Bats: R   Throws: R   Height: 6'2"   Weight: 180
Origin: Round 1, 2018 Draft (#17 overall)

The Report: You can't really blame the Angels for trying their luck again with a toolsy outfielder named Jordy(o)n, given how the last one worked out. There are some differences though, and it's not just the preferred spelling. While I wrote above that Jordon Adell is built like a wideout, Adams actually was a wide receiver, and a highly-rated college recruit as well. While still raw at the plate, he has the quick-twitch wrists to portend a good hit tool although the ultimate power projection is an open question. The athletic tools should allow him to stick in center field and he could be an asset there. This is not something that normally comes into play in our projections but the Angels have done quite well developing these kind of athletic outfield types in recent years, and Adams gives them ideal clay to work with.

The Risks: High. He's still quite raw at the plate, so this is an athleticism bet. It's a whole lotta athleticism at least.

Ben Carsley's Fantasy Take: Are the Angels the new Rangers or something? Adams is one of the more exciting, higher-upside additions to the dynasty player pool. He's likely to be a slow burn type of dude, but if you don't get in on the ground floor now you're likely to miss out altogether. He's a top-101 guy for me already, albeit probably close to the bottom of said list.

6. Matt Thaiss   1B   OFP: 55   Likely: 50
ETA: 2019. The Angels have a bit of a DH/1B glut through 2021 or so.
Born: 05/06/95   Age: 24   Bats: L   Throws: R   Height: 6'0"   Weight: 195
Origin: Round 1, 2016 Draft (#16 overall)

The Report: We usually toss around the term "prospect fatigue" with big name prospects, top 101 guys: J.P. Crawfords, Lewis Brinsons or Nick Gordon. It doesn't feel to me like Matt Thaiss was only drafted two years ago, but the record books say he was; you may remember that Thaiss was one of the two big college catchers in that draft, along with Zack Collins. He immediately shifted to first base, which made him much less interesting as a prospect, but he's hung around an improving Angels Top 10 year-over-year because he's just kept hitting. Some additional power showed up in 2018, although that happens to many 23-year-olds in the PCL. Couple that with a plus hit tool, strong approach, and above-average defense at first and you have... well, there's a reason we've already run out of interesting things to say about him.

The Risks: Low. It's all profile risk here, the bat isn't particularly high variance, although he could use some positive variance in the power column.

Ben Carsley's Fantasy Take: Matt Thaiss has become a bit of a punching bag in the BP dynasty circle—I specifically highlighted my (eventually successful) attempts to sell high on him last year in TDGX—but he's a reasonable asset in deeper leagues. First base isn't quite as flush of a fantasy position as it used to be; Jose Abreu was a top-20 guy last year despite hitting just .265 with 22 homers. Thaiss is capable of matching that output, which will make him a reasonable if unexciting fantasy MI once he's playing every day.

7. Jose Suarez   LHP   OFP: 55   Likely: 50   ETA: 2019
Born: 01/03/98   Age: 21   Bats: L   Throws: L   Height: 5'10"   Weight: 170
Origin: International Free Agent, 2014

The Report: It took Orange County three tries to find an appropriate level for Suarez last year, who embarrassed first High-A, then Double-A hitters in the season's early months. A velocity spike presaged Suarez's coming-out party, as he'll now wander into the mid-90s consistently enough to make a plus-on-its-merits straight change play up all the more. He's aggressive within the zone, moving his fastball around and attacking the hands at will with late life that helps him bust into kitchens and avoid barrels. Occasional issues spotting the pitch periodically landed him in trouble in Triple-A, but he repeats well and projects to have above-average command. His curveball will flash above-average with bat-missing two-plane finishing action at its best, though it is his least consistent pitch at present.

The Risks: The frame is pretty maxed out, and there'll be some conditioning and maintenance concerns as he matures further. There isn't much good projection left here, and the mechanics are already pretty on-brand with his physical signature, so another jump in stuff is unlikely. What he's got already is plenty good, though, which reduces risk considerably. Ongoing development of his hook will go a long way toward determining where in the rotation he lands.

Ben Carsley's Fantasy Take: Suarez is one of my favorite pop-up prospect targets for deep leaguers. There's some Eduardo Rodriguez potential here in terms of the strikeout potential, the lack of consistency, and the potential conditioning issues, but hey now let's get back to those strikeouts. Better yet, Suarez will be ready soon, so he's a good "fail fast" prospect and not a guy you'll need to sit on for three years to figure out who he is. Buy, buy, buy.

8. D'Shawn Knowles   OF
OFP: 55   Likely: 45   ETA: 2023
Born: 01/16/01   Age: 18   Bats: B   Throws: R   Height: 6'0"   Weight: 165
Origin: International Free Agent, 2017

The Report: We keep hammering this point, but the Bahamas are a rapidly emerging market for international talent. Along with Kristian Robinson in the Diamondbacks system, Knowles is at the forefront of the next wave of Bahaman ballplayers. He's an athletic, well-rounded outfield prospect who is reasonably polished for his level of experience. As you can see above, he's hit the ground running in LA's system, getting a stateside assignment at just 17 and continuing to hit when promoted outside the complex.

Knowles is on the smaller, skinnier side—his listed height might be generous but his weight probably isn't. He runs well and projects to stay in center, although we'll always note that players this young and projectable can easily grow out of the middle of the field. It's a sweet swing with some bat speed, and occasionally surprising pop. This all constitutes the makings of a really cool prospect, and he could fly up our lists next year.

The Risks: High, mostly because he was born in 2001 and hasn't played above rookie ball. You can be both high risk and less risky than most of your cohort, I suppose.

Ben Carsley's Fantasy Take: Just a watch-list guy for us, but a fun one! In fact, I'd argue Knowles is a better bet than some of the Rule 4 draft guys you'll start popping in the third or fourth rounds of your new player entry drafts. Especially if those other guys are pitchers.

9. Michael Hermosillo OF
OFP: 50 **Likely:** 45 **ETA:** Debuted in 2018
Born: 01/17/95 Age: 24 Bats: R Throws: R Height: 5'11" Weight: 190
Origin: Round 28, 2013 Draft (#847 overall)

The Report: A veteran of much crappier Angels prospect lists, Hermosillo finally percolated up to the big leagues in 2018. He even earned semi-regular playing time for a few weeks early in the summer and a few more towards the end of September.

A former Illinois running back commit—who subtweeted noted member of the human race Skip Bayless for suggesting Kyler Murray would only be happy on the gridiron—Hermosillo has the general toolsiness and athleticism that you'd expect from someone FBS schools were after to carry the rock. He runs well, throws well, plays the outfield well, and has a reasonable power projection. We do worry about his hit tool playing down due to approach, and he rose through the system very fast and might need some consolidation time at Triple-A.

The Risks: Medium. He might not hit and he's probably not playing much center field in Los Angeles of Anaheim anytime soon. You may have heard of the guy the Angels have out there already.

Ben Carsley's Fantasy Take: Hermosillo could be of interest if he gets regular playing time because of his speed, but until then he is… super not of interest. Please continue to read Baseball Prospectus for our expert dynasty league analysis.

10. Luis Rengifo IF
OFP: 50 **Likely:** 45 **ETA:** 2019
Born: 02/26/97 Age: 22 Bats: B Throws: R Height: 5'10" Weight: 165
Origin: International Free Agent, 2013

The Report: Kudos to the scout(s) who saw it coming; the Halos snagged Rengifo from Tampa in March to complete their trade of C.J. Cron, and all he did was hit, and run, and hit some more, and then run some more. His is a dense frame, packed to the gills with compact muscle and outsized strength, but he retains quick-twitch athleticism in his lower half. The speed is only solid-average, maybe a true 55, but he's nimble in and out of breaks, and his advanced instincts help the speed play up on the bases.

At the dish, he's a switch-hitter with compact actions from both sides. There's comparatively more loft to the right-handed swing, but he's pretty direct and short in both directions. He'll take a lot of pitches, including some he'd probably be better served to attack. But he works himself into good counts on the regular, and coupled with an all-fields approach, he does well to create positive hitting situations and translate them into quality at-bats. There's sneaky average power, but the game utility is geared much more toward the gaps than the fences.

His quickness manifests in impressive lateral agility up the middle, and he has a strong feel for the six with an accurate internal clock and good body control to set up his transfers and throws. The arm strength is okay for the left side, above-average for the keystone, and he has the tools to hold down either position, with above-average leather at the latter.

The Risks: Moderate; the approach can get passive and may be exploited by big-league arms if he doesn't try to drive the ball more. The baserunning value may also continue to dip a little lower against the best batteries, and he's not quite as dynamic a defender as you'd ideally like for that utility role.

Ben Carsley's Fantasy Take: Oh God, it's a fast middle infielder. I can't be trusted with this profile. I… I suggest buying.

The Next Five:

11
Patrick Sandoval   LHP
Born: 10/18/96   Age: 22   Bats: L   Throws: L   Height: 6'3"   Weight: 190
Origin: Round 11, 2015 Draft (#319 overall)

A $900,000 overslot prep once upon a time, Sandoval is still a big, live-armed lefty who got picked up from the Astros at the deadline in the Martin Maldonado trade. He's a bit of a hidden breakout guy because his lines are very split up between promotions and the trade, but he had a brilliant season all-in-all, with midseason promotions from Low-A up to Double-A and plenty of strikeouts to go around. Violence in the delivery points toward a bullpen future. He's a low-90s dude with feel for a curve and the makings of other secondaries, so you'd want him to stay in the rotation, and while there's a lot of reliever risk here, it's not so extreme that it's a fait accompli. Regardless of role, Sandoval will end up being a high price to pay for a half-season of an okay catcher.

12
Ty Buttrey   RHP
Born: 03/31/93   Age: 26   Bats: L   Throws: R   Height: 6'6"   Weight: 230
Origin: Round 4, 2012 Draft (#151 overall)

Buttrey is your classic "Failed starter Day 2 prep arm turned good reliever." He bounced around Red Sox affiliates for five seasons before finally putting it together in the bullpen in 2017. He's taxonomically a "95-and-a-slider" guy, but really more of a "97-and-a-slider guy," and it's a plus slider with good two plane break. He even has enough of a changeup to at least keep it in the back of the batter's mind. It's more eighth inning stuff than closer stuff, but he also might already be the Angels eighth inning guy. There is value in surety, although relievers are rarely a place to find surety, I suppose.

13 Trent Deveaux   OF
Born: 05/04/00   Age: 19   Bats: R   Throws: R   Height: 6'0"   Weight: 160
Origin: International Free Agent, 2017

The 2017 Bahamian class also brought the Angels this fellow, a $1.2 million signee. His pro debut didn't quite go as smoothly as Knowles', as Deveaux was under the Mendoza line in complex league ball. It's questionable whether we should even be keeping stats in that league, let alone paying particularly close attention to them, and a stateside assignment as a first-year pro is, itself, actually somewhat promising. We did repeatedly hear good things about his athleticism and speed—you have probably discerned by now that the Angels have a type here—and it's a projectable body. We just don't know whether he's going to hit quite yet.

14 Chris Rodriguez   RHP
Born: 07/20/98   Age: 20   Bats: R   Throws: R   Height: 6'2"   Weight: 185
Origin: Round 4, 2016 Draft (#126 overall)

Rodriguez missed all of 2018 with a back injury. I'm familiar enough with the level of hushed tones required for various arm injuries, but back issues leave me a bit nonplussed. The most recent good pitching prospects with back issues I can think of are Kolby Allard, AJ Puk, and Thomas Szapucki. One of them lost a bunch of velocity—although not immediately—and the other two are currently rehabbing from Tommy John. Hardly a significant sample, and hardly enough information on Rodriguez to feel confident in any sort of 2019 projection. What I do know was I expected him to be up with the Top 101 types in the top five by this point, and while the injury injects a fair bit of uncertainty, I don't know that it dings the upside as much.

15 Livan Soto   SS
Born: 06/22/00   Age: 19   Bats: L   Throws: R   Height: 6'0"   Weight: 160
Origin: International Free Agent, 2017

The other guy the Angels signed out of the Braves international prospect scandal might now be the best prospect. Soto got $850,000 from the Angels late in 2017 to pair with his $1,000,000 from the Braves. He's not a particularly physical player—there's literally no present power here and not a ton of projection, and he's not speedy either. He does have contact skills and precocious control of the strike zone given his age, and he has good defensive ability. The question is whether his lack of impact athleticism and potential physical growth might push him off the 6. He was already playing a fair amount of second at Orem.

Others of note:

Kevin Maitan, 3B/SS, Short-Season Orem

For years, Maitan was considered the best player in the world in his age group. The Braves locked him up early in the 2016 pool—far, far earlier than they were allowed—for $4.25 million, and then he got another $2.2 million from the Angels when the league made him a free agent. The problem is that, in the period between when Atlanta locked him up and when he actually started playing professionally, it sure seems like his baseball skills deteriorated a lot. He's gotten big and slow, and he hasn't hit much either. There's still bat speed and some latent interesting hitting ability, but it's a long swing and it's already getting exploited by low-level pitchers. It's too early to give up—he did get that $2.2 million just a year ago—but we're officially worried now.

Top Talents 25 and Under (born 4/1/93 or later):

1. Shohei Ohtani
2. Jo Adell
3. Griffin Canning
4. Jahmai Jones
5. Brandon Marsh
6. Jordyn Adams
7. David Fletcher
8. Jaime Barria
9. Matt Thaiss
10. Jose Suarez

Tommy John surgery is just a bummer, straight-up. It sucks when it robs us of the opportunity to watch special pitchers do special things, and it sucks when it blunts burgeoning careers before they can become special. Luckily for us all, at least Shohei Ohtani can hit really well, too. For all the gnashing of teeth about holes awaiting exposure by big-league stuff last spring, the young phenom more than held his own in his first taste of the world's best pitching, to the tune of a 122 DRC+ and one of the best barrel rates in baseball. He's not going to throw many more pitches while still eligible for this list, but that doesn't stop him from holding some of the highest 25U value in the game, both on the field and off.

It's difficult to believe we're here and admitting as much, but I think we're still undervaluing David Fletcher. In his first taste of The Show he sparkplugged a whole heap of defensive value all over the dirt, his wheels and aggressiveness played well on the bases, and he held his own against big-league arms. That's a recipe for a long career, and at least the earliest returns indicate that he deserves a bit more love.

Pressed into urgent service earlier than expected, Jaime Barria responded with acceptable topline production across nearly 130 innings, even as the DRA warning light flashed with furious urgency throughout. The overperformance to underlying metrics isn't especially surprising given the profile, and the stuff played basically as advertised. It's an archetype that tends to garner more doubt than benefit thereof, as middling velocity and 90th-percentile results in launch angles and batted ball distances allowed tends to be an awfully tough mix to sustain. Barria's deception and strong command affords more optimism than usual, but the ceiling remains fairly well-defined.

The rest of this list reiterates just how far Anaheim's system has come in a relatively short time. This is a franchise, after all, that just two winters ago sat 29th on our organizational rankings with a single, solitary BP101er. That guy's still going to feature on this year's list, along with at least three organization mates, and with swells of interesting, tooled-up youngin's at the complex level it's now a system capable of adding more high-end volume to the ranks right quick.

Part 3: Featured Articles

The Hole in The Shift is Fixing Itself

Russell Carleton

I've been on a bit of a mission against The Shift of late. I'm not out to get The Shift for the usual reasons that people oppose it. The words "the right way to play the game" won't be found on my lips. If a team wants to pursue a strategy that is within the rules and it works, then by all means, they have my blessing (not that they need it). Instead, my concern with The Shift is a worry that it doesn't work, or at least that it has a flaw that needs fixing.

The data show that while The Shift does a decent job of preventing singles on balls in play (what it's supposed to do), it also increases the number of walks that happen in front of it, and the number of additional walks outweighs the number of singles saved. It's a problem because you can't throw a guy out if he gets to walk to first base.

But the "why" was important. It seemed that The Shift was changing the way in which pitchers pitched. We saw that there were fewer fastballs thrown in front of The Shift than we might otherwise expect, and that pitchers tended to stay out of the strike zone a little more. Not by a lot. In fact, it might not even be visible to the naked eye. The percentage of pitches that are out of the zone goes from 51.0 to 53.3 from a standard defense (two right/two left) to a full shift (three on one side). That difference stands up even after we control for the types of hitters that get shifted against. And it's enough to drive up the walk rate to where it cancels out the benefits that teams thought they were getting with The Shift... and then some.

But there was some hope. I found that when individual pitchers stayed closer to the in-zone/out-of-zone mix that they used without The Shift on, they could still get the benefits of The Shift without the walk problems. So, in theory, a team could simply figure out a way to convince its pitchers to not fall prey to the walk trap and The Shift would once again be their friend.

It's reasonable to think that some teams might be more hip to this idea than others. Maybe some figured it out a year before the others. Maybe they were better at getting the message across to their pitchers. Or, maybe no one has figured it out yet.

Warning! Gory Mathematical Details Ahead!

I used data from 2015-2017, made available through MLB's data portal, Baseball Savant. They are kind enough to note when teams are using an infield shift (three fielders on one side of second base), as opposed to a "strategic shift" (someone's playing a bit out of position, but it's not quite that drastic) or a "standard" alignment.

Since we're doing this by team, I can't just look at raw walk rates, because we know that some teams have good pitchers and others have not-so-good pitchers. Some have a mix of both. I used the log-odds ratio method to take into account a batter's general walking proclivities, and a pitcher's as well, and then shoving them into a binary logistic regression. Then, I asked the computer to generate a specific coefficient for each team's pitchers, for when they went into The Shift and how that affected their walk rate.

Using those coefficients, I was able to project what would happen if a league-average pitcher faced a league-average hitter (which we expect would product a league-average walk rate; from 2015-2017, 7.7 percent of plate appearances ended in a walk) and then just switched his hat. Here's the top five and the bottom five:

Top 5 Teams	Projected Shift Walk Rate	Bottom 5 Teams	Projected Shift Walk Rate
Rockies	6.2%	Rangers	11.2%
Pirates	6.7%	Mets	10.4%
Indians	7.2%	Dodgers	10.2%
Astros	7.3%	Cardinals	9.9%
Braves	7.7%	Tigers	9.7%

There are probably people out there right now trying to figure out what the common thread is among the top and bottom teams. I'm sure, because this is Baseball Prospectus, people are already trying to make the case that sabermetric "early adopters" have some sort of edge here. I think that the more interesting piece is that by the time you get to fifth place in The Shift, we're at league average.

As a sanity check, I examined the issue on a pitch-by-pitch level, looking at how often pitchers threw their pitches in the GameDay strike zone, and again using the same basic methodology and getting team-specific coefficients. The names on the list re-arranged themselves, but the idea was the same, and the two lists correlated with an R of .593.

There's a reason that I don't usually do this type of leaderboard post. I don't really know what the Rockies, Pirates, Indians, Astros, and Braves have in common, or what they have that the bottom five don't. I can put a shrug emoji here and say, "Well, it must be something!" but that seems like a cop-out. Instead, I'd like to present another table and suggest that the table above doesn't even really matter anymore.

Year	League Percent Outside K Zone (Full Shift)	League Percent in K Zone (No Shift)	Difference
2015	54.1%	51.1%	3.0%
2016	53.3%	50.9%	2.4%
2017	52.6%	50.9%	1.7%
2018	52.0%	50.7%	1.3%

The hole in The Shift is fixing itself, and it's coming down really fast league wide. In my earlier work on The Shift, I suggested that until teams stopped having such a huge difference between their out-of-zone rate with and without The Shift on, there would just be too many walks for The Shift to make sense. It seems that all 30 of them have been working toward just that. I once estimated that it takes about 10 years for an idea to filter its way through baseball. At this rate, it looks like teams are going to catch up a lot faster than that. And yeah, they're all saber-smart now.

It's likely that whatever magic it was that the Rockies and Pirates had has made its way to Texas and Queens. Or is at least on its way. And if teams are committing to fixing the walk problem, then it's likely that they will continue shifting and shifting a lot.

And eventually it's going to actually make sense for them to do it.

—*Russell Carleton is a former author of Baseball Prospectus and now an analyst for the New York Mets.*

The State of the Quality Start

Rob Mains

One of the seven things you (probably) didn't know about the 2018 season is that quality starts—defined as a start lasting six or more innings with three or fewer earned runs allowed—as a percentage of total starts cratered to an all-time low of 41 percent. I want to look a little more deeply into this, since it's been a while (May of 2016, to be exact) since I've examined quality starts.

The term *quality start* is credited to *Philadelphia Inquirer* sportswriter John Lowe. It's been derided ever since he coined it in December of 1985. Three runs in six innings? That's a 4.50 ERA! In what world is that a measure of quality?

Let's start with that criticism. It's true that 3 x 9 / 6 = 4.5. (You came here for this sort of high-level math, right?) But it's also true that type of start, meeting the bare minimum for earning a quality start, is unusual. Here's the proportion of quality starts in which the pitcher lasted exactly six innings and yielded exactly three earned runs. (I'm going to confine this analysis to the 30-team era, 1998-present. Almost all data retrieved in this article is via the Baseball-Reference Play Index.)

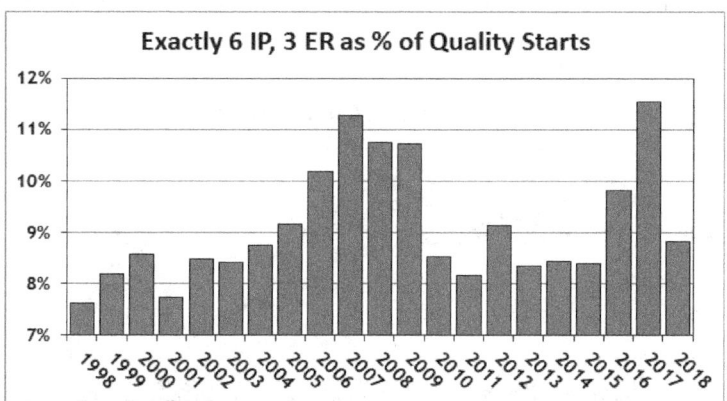

There were 1,997 quality starts in 2018. Only 176, or fewer than one in 11, featured a pitcher going six innings and allowing three earned runs. Put another way, the percentage of quality starts that resulted in a 4.50 ERA (8.8 percent) is less than half the percentage of games in which a batter hit two home runs and his team lost (22.5 percent; 237-69 won-lost). That doesn't impugn hitting two homers.

So if a 4.50 ERA isn't the norm, what is? How good are quality starts?

Pretty good, it turns out. First, on a team level:

Teams receiving a quality start from their pitcher won 68.4 percent of their games in 2018, in line with the 30-team era average of 67.9 percent. A team with a .684 winning percentage wins 111 games. Getting a quality start is definitely a good thing. Individual pitchers throwing quality starts have a higher winning percentage because a big slice of team losses is assigned to a reliever.

If teams do well in quality starts, how well do the starting pitchers do? Again, very well.

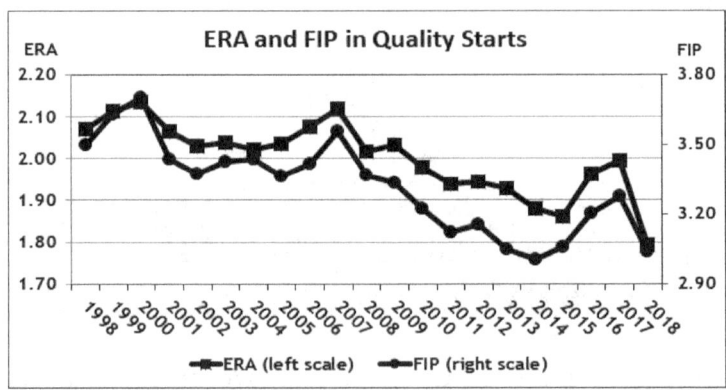

Pitchers in quality starts had a 1.79 ERA (blue line) in 2018, *the lowest in the 30-team era*. Their FIP was higher, 3.04, but still excellent. In the 30-team era, only 2014 had a lower FIP for quality starts, 3.01.

But, of course, the run environment in 2014 was different. Teams in 2014 scored 4.07 runs per game, the fewest in a non-strike year since 1976. They scored 4.45 runs per game in 2018. So surrendering a 3.04 FIP in 2018 is more impressive than 3.01 in 2014. Accordingly, let's look at ERA and FIP in quality starts relative to league averages.

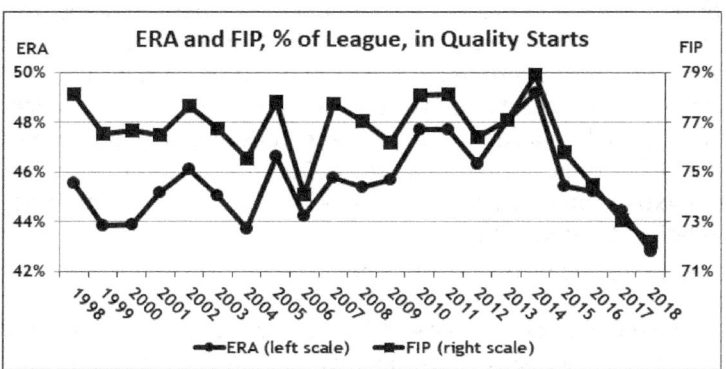

This tells a more dramatic story. Starting pitchers in 2018 gave up a 4.19 ERA and a 4.21 FIP. Starters in quality starts gave up a 1.79 ERA, 43 percent of the league average. Starters in quality starts gave up a 3.04 FIP, 72 percent of the league average. Both of these marks represent lows in the 30-team era.

The takeaway here is this: *Quality starts are better, relative to other starts, than they've ever been over the past 21 years.*

Maybe during the winter I'll look at this over a longer arc of time. For now, though, we can definitively say quality starts are the best they've ever been since the Diamondbacks and Rays joined the majors.

Yet, paradoxically, they're down.

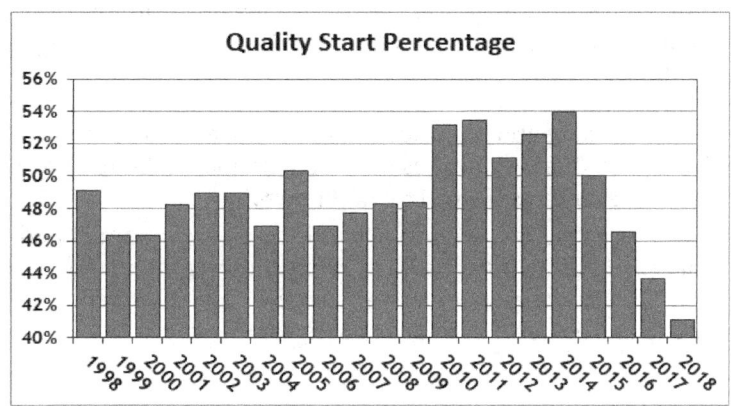

This graph covers only the 30-team era. In my article last week, though, I looked at the years 1908-2018. The result was the same. The 41 percent of starts in 2018 that were quality starts are an all-time low, well below the runners-up: 1930's 43 percent (the year teams scored an all-time record 5.55 runs per game) and last year's 44 percent.

The normal explanation for a dip in quality start percentage is an increase in scoring. When teams score a lot of runs, it's harder for starting pitchers to last six or more innings and limit opponents to three earned runs. From 1998 to 2014, the correlation between runs scored per game and the percentage of starts that were quality starts was -0.94. That means there was an extremely close relationship: More runs, fewer quality starts. Too small a sample? Go back to the start of the Expansion Era, 1961, and the relationship is even more negative, a -0.95 correlation, though 2014.

But that's broken down over the past four years:

- 2015: Runs per game increased from 4.07 to 4.25, quality start percentage decreased from 54.0 to 50.1. Yes, that's a negative relationship, but the regression model would predict a decline of 1.5 percentage points. We got 3.9 instead.
- 2016: Runs per game increased from 4.25 to 4.48, quality start percentage decreased from 50.1 to 46.6. Past experience would suggest a decline of just 1.8 percentage points. We got 3.4.
- 2017: Runs per game increased from 4.48 to 4.65, quality start percentage decreased from 46.6 to 43.6. Again, the direction's right, but the magnitude isn't. Using the relationship from 1998 to 2014, that increase in scoring should've reduced quality starts by 1.3 percentage points, not 2.9.
- 2018: Runs per game declined from 4.65 to 4.45. That should've resulted in the quality start percentage moving in the other direction, rising 1.6 points. It didn't. It fell 2.6 points, as noted, to an all-time low.

Granted, we're talking about just four years here. Maybe they're outliers. But I don't think they are. Quality starts, as noted, are as good or better than ever. But they're rarer than ever as well. And I think I know why.

To get a quality start, you need to allow three or fewer earned and pitch at least six innings. That's 18 outs. Here's a graph showing the number of starting pitchers who limited their opponents to three or fewer earned runs but got pulled after pitching at least five innings but fewer than six:

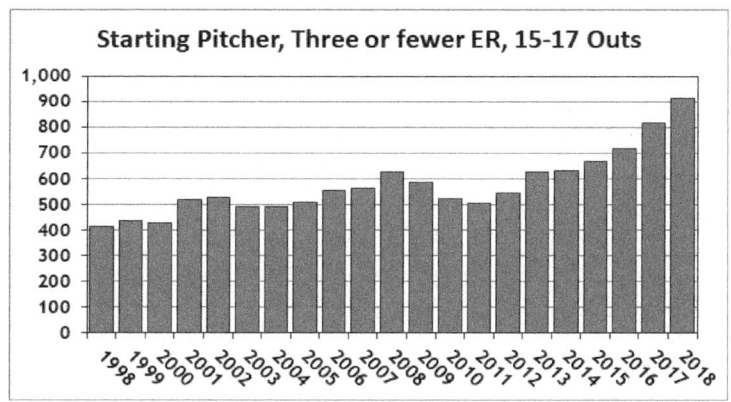

A pitcher getting 15 outs pitched five innings. A pitcher getting 16 outs pitched 5 1/3. A pitcher getting 17 outs pitched 5 2/3. More than ever before, pitchers are being removed from games in which they are within 1-3 outs of a quality start, falling just short of the six-inning finish line. Widespread acknowledgement of the times-through-the-order penalty and a flotilla of available bullpen arms is making the quality start simultaneously both more excellent and more rare.

Which is ironic, given that we saw a new post-war quality start record this season:

Rank	Pitcher	Season	Consecutive QS
1	Jacob deGrom	2018	24
2	Bob Gibson	1968	22
-	Chris Carpenter	2005	22
4	Johan Santana	2004	21
5	Luis Tiant	1968	20
-	Mike Scott	1986	20
-	Jake Arrieta	2015	20
8	Robin Roberts	1952	19
-	Tom Seaver	1973	19
-	Jack Morris	1983	19
-	Greg Maddux	1998	19
-	Josh Johnson	2010	19
-	Jon Lester	2014	19

While there have been longer streaks spread over multiple seasons, no pitcher since World War II threw more consecutive quality starts in one year than Jacob deGrom this year. The fact that he did in a year in which quality starts were the rarest they've ever been adds to the accomplishment.

—Rob Mains is an author of Baseball Prospectus.

Heads-Up Hacking—The First Pitch

Matthew Trueblood

Batters fell behind in a higher percentage of all plate appearances in 2018 than in any previous season for which we have pitch-by-pitch data. That kind of granular information goes back only to 1988, but we might safely assume (given all we know about baseball as it had been before that, and as it has been in the years since) that batters have *never* fallen behind at a higher rate than they did last season.

Through the 1990s, the percentage of all plate appearances that began 0-1 hovered in the high 30s and low 40s. In the 2000s, it rose steadily but slowly, through the mid-40s. In 2018, 49.8 percent of all trips to the plate began 0-1. That, as much as anything, captures in microcosm the nature of hitting in MLB today.

A countdown clock toward strike three begins ticking almost the moment a batter takes his place in the box. The league's adjusted OPS+ on the first pitch was higher in 2018 than ever before, and that has been true in most of the last 10 seasons. Batters hit .264/.289/.442 in all plate appearances in which they swung at the first pitch last season, and .241/.330/.395 in all plate appearances in which they took that first offering.

The percentage differences in batting average and isolated power there favor swinging at the first pitch by more than in any season since 1988, while the difference in on-base percentage favors taking by more than ever. If you want to get on base at a decent clip, it's a good idea to be patient, but you run the risk of missing the only chances you'll get to produce power.

Los Angeles Angels 2019

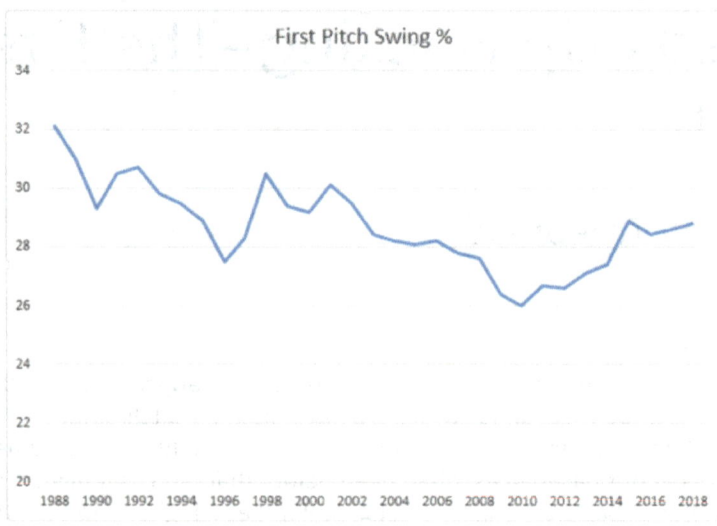

The league swung at the first pitch 28.8 percent of the time in 2018. With the isolated exception of 2015, that's the highest that number has climbed since 2002, but it might not be high enough. With the help of BP research maven Rob McQuown, I looked at the aggregate Called Strike Probability (CSProb) on the first pitch for each season since 2008, when the implementation of PITCHf/x first made measuring that possible. It's risen sharply during that period.

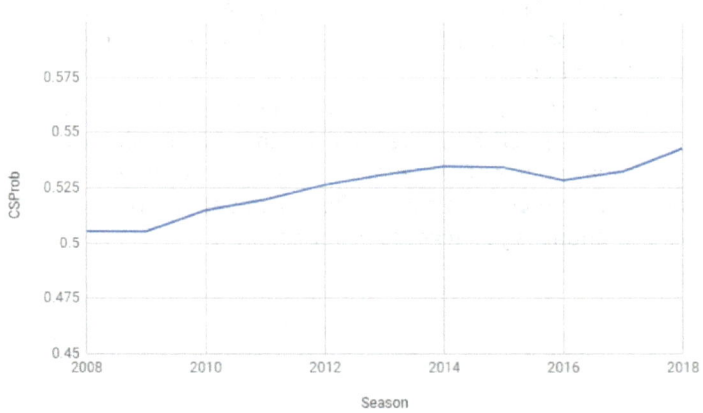

Called Strike Probability, First Pitch of PA (2008-2018)

Called Strike Probability is exactly what it sounds like: a pitch with a given CSProb has roughly that chance of being called a strike, if not swung at. In 2018, a batter who took 100 first pitches from a random sampling of the league's pitchers might expect to fall behind 54 or 55 times—up from 50 or 51 times in 2008. Almost regardless of pitch type (and, notably, especially in the case of fastballs), the first pitch tends to have more of the zone right now than ever before.

Pitchers are better at throwing strikes. They have better stuff, and believe more in their ability to miss bats within the zone. Perhaps most importantly, they know that batters are looking for one thing on the first pitch: a fastball. If they don't get it, they're likely to take the pitch. Check out how the use of sinkers and four-seamers on the first pitch has changed in a decade:

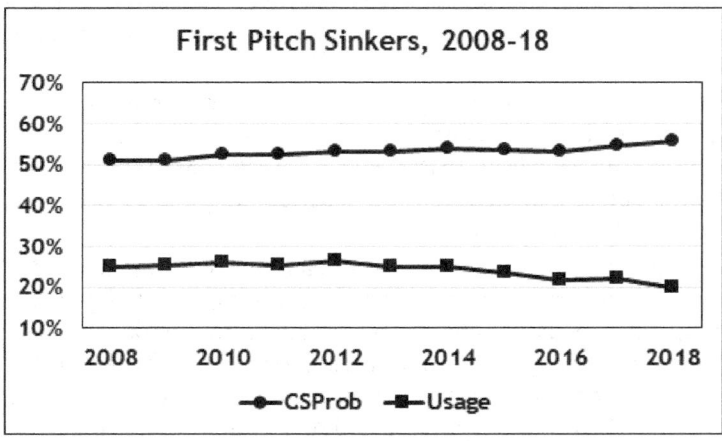

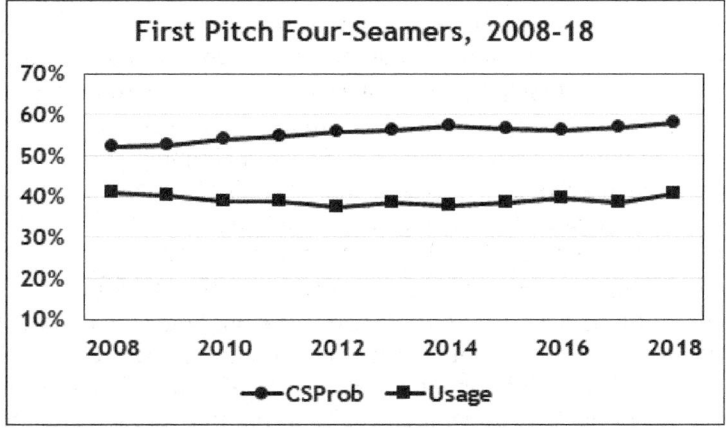

The sinker is losing its place in baseball, but the rate at which pitchers have thrown it on the first pitch hasn't dropped any faster than its usage rate in other counts. Pitchers have actually gone to their four-seamer *more* often to open counts, in the last few years, after a dip in the 2012-2015 period. What's really changed, though, and what shows up in both charts above, is that pitchers are catching more of the zone with first-pitch fastballs than they were a decade ago, or a half-decade ago. They're attacking right away, even with the pitch they know batters are expecting. The message is pretty clear: batters are being too passive.

Sliders, curves, and changeups each have more of the zone when thrown on the first pitch than they did several years ago, too, though the effect is less pronounced. Pitchers have seen the numbers; they know batters are doing better on the first pitch itself. They still feel safe throwing more and better strikes than ever before, figuring they'll come out ahead as long as they keep getting ahead to open each battle.

The Moneyball revolution brought an increased league-wide focus on OBP, which resulted in a de facto mandate to take a more patient tack at the plate. It worked very well for a while, as batters with poor plate discipline were compelled to either adjust or be expelled from the league, and pitchers with poor control were slowly weeded out.

However, concurrent with that revolution, and spurred by it in some ways, was the evolution of the pitching paradigm that now dominates the game. As batters ratcheted up their focus on inflating pitch counts and working walks, pitchers honed theirs on throwing strikes and missing bats. The league's understanding of what makes a good pitcher improved at least as much, from the mid-1990s through the mid-2000s, as its understanding of what makes a good hitter. As amphetamines and other performance-enhancing drugs were phased mostly out of the game, and as PITCHf/x broke onto the scene, individuals and teams learned how to exploit the evolved approaches of even the smartest hitters.

The ability to avoid making outs is still the most valuable one in baseball, but the magnitude of its eclipse of slugging is smaller than ever. To a greater extent than power, on-base skills derive their value from chaining—from the on-base skill levels of the players on either side of a given individual. Eleven years ago, when the housing crisis hit, people learned the hard way that the value of their homes depended a good deal on the values of their neighbors' homes. The same wasn't true, though, of their cars. So it is now, with OBP and SLG.

The global OBP in 2018 was .318. The only seasons since the Dead Ball Era in which the league got on base at a worse clip were 2013-2015, 1988, 1971-1972, and 1963-1968. This is all happening despite the aforementioned evolution of the science of hitting. It's happening despite a shift in approach and focus, one that would steer OBP ever higher, if only it were working.

Instead, it's sitting at a low ebb, and while it does so, even guys who get on base often are a little less helpful than they were 10 years ago—or 20, or 40, or 60, or 70, or 80, or 90. They're less helpful, that is, because unless there happen to be three or four other guys in the lineup who get on just as regularly, their contribution is merely to forestall the inevitable. Runs happen, increasingly, when a sudden bang happens, and that means attacking early in the count—because pitchers are sure as hell doing that.

In a league making contact on barely 75 percent of its swings, and a league in which an increasing number of pitchers can throw multiple off-speed pitches for strikes in any count, the only way to consistently generate offense is going to be aggressive. This isn't necessarily true for individuals, like Mookie Betts and Jose Ramirez, who make a lot of contact and have excellent plate discipline, and whose power comes from such natural quickness in a short stroke. Most players have to make tradeoffs, though, whether it be lowering their contact rate or raising their chase rate, in order to consistently make the quality of contact necessary to survive in today's game.

Highest %	Lowest %
Javier Baez – 48.3	Joe Mauer – 4.6
Freddie Freeman – 47.1	Mookie Betts – 9.7
Ozzie Albies – 46.3	Brett Gardner – 10.7
Jose Altuve – 44.2	Jose Ramirez – 12.0
Nick Castellanos – 44.1	Jason Kipnis – 13.8
Joey Gallo – 42.3	Jesus Aguilar – 14.5
Corey Dickerson – 40.9	Xander Bogaerts – 15.8
Salvador Perez – 40.8	Brian Dozier – 16.3
Eddie Rosario – 40.7	Mike Trout – 17.6
Nick Ahmed – 40.4	Yasmani Grandal – 17.6

Top 10 and Bottom 10 Hitters, First-Pitch Swing Rate (2018)

The question isn't which of these lists one prefers, but what they each convey, qualitatively, about the cat-and-mouse game of early-count hitting. Those top five on the left, especially, drive home the fact that for most players, getting aggressive early in the count is now key to keeping strikeout rate down and hitting for power.

For now, the message is: pitchers are coming right after batters with the nastiest stuff they've ever had. Batters had better stop giving away strike one and force hurlers to adjust, or the global OBP crisis is only going to get worse.

—*Matthew Trueblood is an author of Baseball Prospectus.*

A Hymn for the Index Stat

Patrick Dubuque

We survived without computers. I know this, because I remember the day when my dad hooked up his brand-new Atari 400 computer to the back of our 12-inch Magnavox television, and the perfect blue of the memo pad lit up for the first time. I was born just on the edge of that transitional generation, of learning cursive and balancing checkbooks and just doing math all the time, constant manual arithmetic.

It still amazes me. We learned how to sail ships without computers. We learned how to do calculus. We built towers that didn't fall down, most of the time. We engineered catapults to knock them down anyway. We built a robust system of philosophy called "utilitarianism," founded on the principle that the good of an action is evaluated by summing the effects of that action, which is the kind of formula that would make the world's mainframes crash. The whole foundation of statistics as a field is "here's math you could easily do but would die of old age first."

The fact of the matter is that there is too much math in the world to do. There are too many things changing, and too many things too small to notice, for us to handle. At some point, they become too much for the computers to handle as well, which is why we have chaos theory and undetectable earthquakes, but it's not an even fight. At some point, we fall back on intuition, and given how under-equipped we are, we're forced to bestow that intuition with some sort of supernatural superiority, the "gut feeling," that we can't prove because we can only intuit that our intuition is better.

We're all lousy at intuition, and wonderful at lying to ourselves about it. The honest truth is that computers are far better at intuition than we are, because in order to know what feels "off" you have to know what's "on." In order to do that you have to constantly reassess the average of everything, then re-rank your own experience against it.

Test your own, by comparing these three anonymous lines:

Player	G	HR	AVG	OBP	SLG
Player A	156	38	.259	.342	.535
Player B	154	38	.280	.348	.527
Player C	158	38	.266	.343	.509

These all seem like pretty similar players, right? The second one a touch more batted-ball dependent, the third a little less strong, but all pretty good hitters. And you'd be right, about the latter. Not the former.

Here's the breakdown:

- Player A: 1991 Howard Johnson, 141 DRC+
- Player B: 1996 Dean Palmer, 121 DRC+
- Player C: 2018 Giancarlo Stanton, 114 DRC+

Baseball is fortunate to have escaped the seismic shifts of so many other sports, where the talents and performances of other eras are nearly unrecognizable. (And not just other sports: try to explain the greatness of the movie Duck Soup without adjusting for era.) But they're still there, and they're nearly impossible to account for manually, without having to resort to sweeping generalizations like "steroid era" or juiced-ball era" to throw out entire swathes of production.

This is all to say that we should celebrate the index stat, that simple 100-based scale with such a humble aim: just to give context. It's hard to imagine how we lived without them for so long. Sabermetricians have always tried to make their stats look like other stats: True Average mapped to batting average, FIP molded to look like and compare to ERA. It's easy to understand the motivation—these statistics carry an emotional value in them that is hard to resist, as with the .300 hitter and the 2.00 ERA—but even they fall prey to the same loss of scale as their unadjusted counterparts. If a .300 average means different things in different years, does that hold true for a .300 True Average?

Instead, 100 doesn't say anything, except above average or below. And it does it instantly, for every season in every run environment for any statistic we want it to. We should have more index stats: K%+, so we can stop comparing Mike Clevinger's career 9.46 K/9 to Nolan Ryan's 9.55. HBP%+, so we can note that Ron Hunt was getting plunked when nobody else was getting plunked, as opposed to that imitator Brandon Guyer. Some might note how stale these references are and accuse league-adjustment as a backward-looking drive, and this is true. But we're always looking backward, always comparing the new with the expectations already set. The index stat just forces us to be honest.

There's always resistance to a new statistic, especially one so outwardly simple and so internally complex. We tend to stick with what we know, even in the case of formulas that are supposed to tell us what we know. But if your resistance is that it seems too complicated, too counterintuitive, too "black boxy," I encourage you to consider why you feel that way. Because the real world is infinitely more complicated than baseball, where all the pitches go in one basic direction and the baserunners are only allowed to travel in four directions. Baseball statistics based on mixed methodology are almost impossibly intricate. So are skyscrapers and automobiles. That's why we have computers—to take the guesswork out of them.

—*Patrick Dubuque is an author of Baseball Prospectus.*

Index of Names

Adams, Jordyn 84, 106
Adell, Jo 85, 103
Allen, Cody 48
Almonte, Miguel 100
Anderson, Justin 50
Barria, Jaime 52
Beasley, Jeremy 94
Bedrosian, Cam 54
Bour, Justin 22
Bourjos, Peter 99
Briceno, Jose 99
Buttrey, Ty 56, 110
Cahill, Trevor 58
Calhoun, Kole 24
Canning, Griffin 95, 104
Castillo, Jesus 100
Cole, Taylor 60
Cowart, Kaleb 99
Cozart, Zack 26
Curtiss, John 100
Deveaux, Trent 99, 111
English, William 99
Fletcher, David 28
Garcia, Luis 62
Garneau, Dustin 99
Harvey, Matt 64
Heaney, Andrew 66
Hermosillo, Michael 30, 109
Hudson, Daniel 68
Jackson, Jeremiah 86
Jennings, Dan 100
Jerez, Williams 100
Jewell, Jake 100
Jones, Jahmai 87, 105
Knowles, D'Shawn 88, 108
La Stella, Tommy 32
Lucroy, Jonathan 34
Madero, Luis 100
Maitan, Kevin 89, 111
Marsh, Brandon 90, 105
Middleton, Keynan 70
Ohtani, Shohei 72, 91
Pena, Felix 74
Peters, Dillon 100
Pujols, Albert 36
Ramirez, J.C. 100
Ramirez, Noe 76
Rengifo, Luis 92, 109
Robles, Hansel 78
Rodriguez, Chris 111
Sandoval, Patrick 96, 110
Simmons, Andrelton 38
Skaggs, Tyler 80
Smith, Kevan 40
Soriano, Jose 97
Soto, Livan 99, 111
Suarez, Jose 98, 107
Thaiss, Matt 93, 107
Tropeano, Nick 82
Trout, Mike 42
Upton, Justin 44
Walsh, Jared 99

Los Angeles Angels 2019

Ward, Taylor 46

Ballpark diagrams for Baseball Prospectus are created by THIRTY81Project, a design concept offering original ballpark artwork, including the new 'Ballparks of 2019' 11 x 17 color print.

Visit **www.thirty81project.com** for full details.

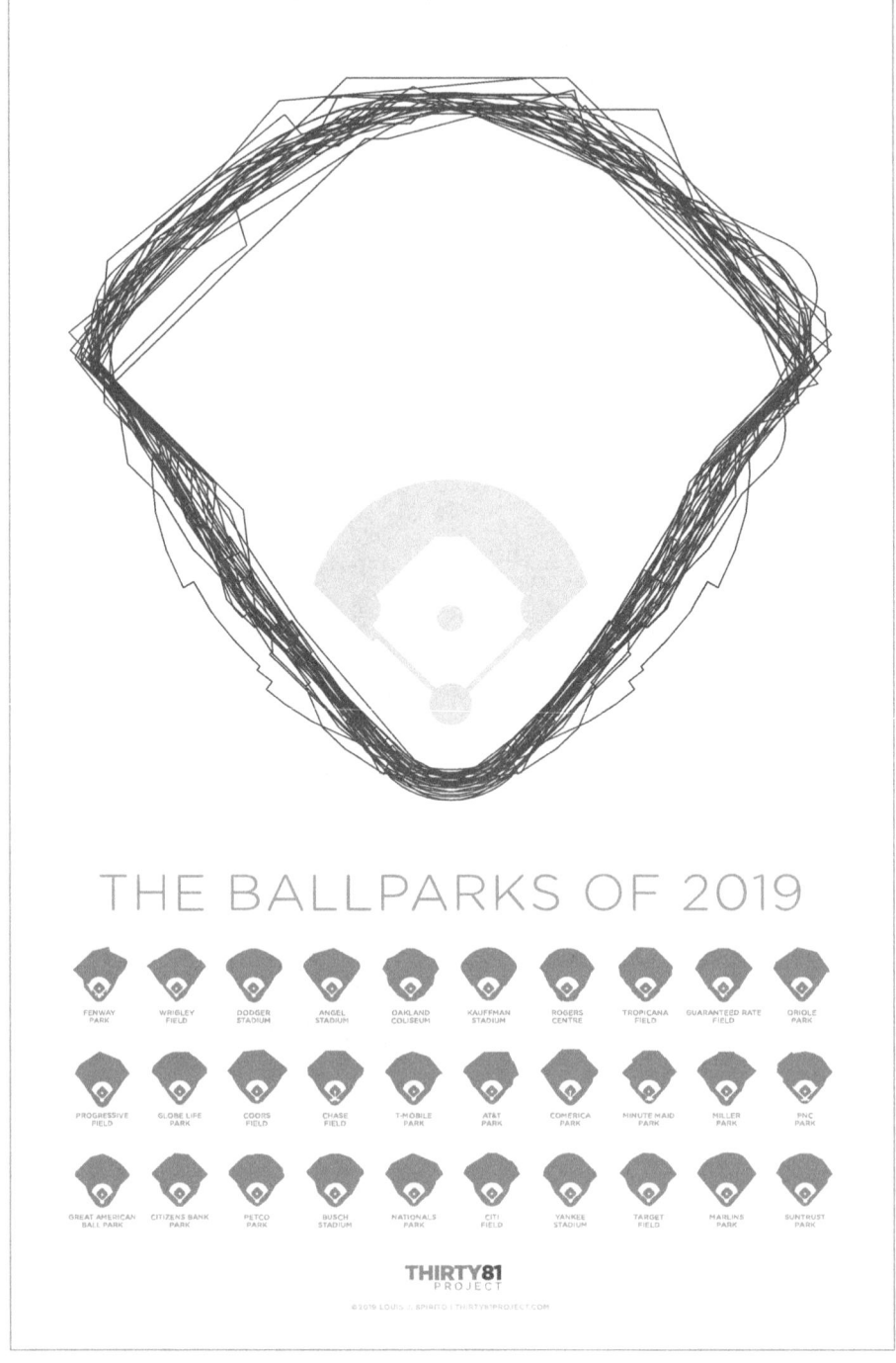